Freeman Edwin Miller

Songs from the South-west Country

Freeman Edwin Miller

Songs from the South-west Country

ISBN/EAN: 9783744766883

Printed in Europe, USA, Canada, Australia, Japan

Cover: Foto ©Thomas Meinert / pixelio.de

More available books at **www.hansebooks.com**

CAPTAIN D. L. PAYNE.

These are his meeds: Homes fill the plains
Where he, a martyr, walked in chains,
* * * * * * * *
And every place where once he stood
Proclaims the glories of his good !

Songs from the Southwest Country

By Freeman E. Miller, A. M.

Author of "Oklahoma, and Other Poems," etc.;
Professor of the English Language and Literature in
the Oklahoma Agricultural and Mechanical College

New York
The Knickerbocker Press
1899

COPYRIGHT, 1898
BY
FREEMAN E. MILLER
All Rights Reserved

To
His Excellency
Hon. CASSIUS M. BARNES
Governor of Oklahoma Territory
Whose Life has been Given to the Development
of the Southwest Country and to whose Heart that
Favored Land is as Dear as an Only Child
This Volume is Respectfully
Inscribed

920837

I never doubt the songs we sing
    Through all the ages grow in grace,
Till in their angel anthems ring
    The loves and longings of the race;
They treasure up for deafened ears
The murmurs of the cycled years,
Till at the last in music roll
Their thunders through the mystic soul!

The most of the poems in this volume are printed here for the first time; several, however, have appeared in the *Century Magazine*, the *Youth's Companion*, *Peterson's Magazine*, the *Bachelor of Arts*, the *Overland Monthly*, and other copyrighted publications; and to their editors thanks are hereby given for permission to reprint.

CONTENTS.

CAPTAIN PAYNE AND HIS HOME IN OKLAHOMA,
Frontispiece.

	PAGE
THE SOUTHWEST COUNTRY	xi

SONGS FROM THE SOUTHWEST COUNTRY.

	PAGE
THE OPENING OF OKLAHOMA:	
AT MORNING,—THE DESERT LAND	1
AT NOON,—THE RACE FOR HOMES	3
AT NIGHT,—THE DESERT CONQUERED	7
THE BALLAD OF THE ALAMO	9
THE BATTLE OF THE WASHITA	19
THE PLAINT OF THE TENDERFOOT	27
SLAUGHTERING THE PONIES	32
DAVID L. PAYNE	36
KANSAS	39
THE STAMPEDE	42
A SONG FOR THE SETTLER	45
LINES ON CAPTAIN PAYNE'S CABIN	47
MOUNTAIN SONG	48
"WHEN THE GOLDEN-ROD IS YELLOW"	49
ON THE SHANKY-TANK	50
OKLAHOMA	52
THE MISSISSIPPI	52
THE PLAINS	53
BY THE OVERLAND TRAIL	54
"WHERE CUSTER FELL"	54

Contents.

	PAGE
THE COWBOY POET	55
THE SUNFLOWER	55

SONNETS.

BOOKS	59
THE TEACHER	59
ON THE GREAT PYRAMID	60
IN A PUBLIC LIBRARY	61
AT ROSSETTI'S GRAVE	61
NEW ENGLAND	62
IMMUTABLE	63
THE MIGHTIEST	63
LILITH	64
ABSENT	65
PREOCCUPIED	65
A DREAM	66
TO ——	67
TO ——	67
THE ONE WHO UNDERSTANDS	68
SYMPATHY	69
UNFORGETTING	69
THE DOOR OF LIFE	70
INACTION	71
TO THE RESCUE	72

MISCELLANEOUS.

AT EASTERTIDE	75
THE OLD RANGE ROAD	79
THE NIGHT	85
"O MY HEART, BE BRAVE AGAIN!"	88
CREEDS	90
THE CONQUEROR	93
IMMORTAL	95
MIND	96
DREAMER AND SINGER	98
THE ROSES	100

Contents.

	PAGE
GREED	102
PLAYING HORSE	104
A GLAD PLAYFELLOW	106
THE ON-MARCH	108
THE DREAMER	110
THE STARS	112
THE LITTLE BOY'S HAIR	113
THE LITTLE DEAD BABY	115
RENUNCIATION	117
"THERE, MY HEART, BE STILL A MINUTE"	118
A RAMBLE	120
UNFORGETTING	121
THE MINOR CHORD	123
IN THE NIGHT	124
SAVE THE BOYS	127
TAKE IT EASY	128
MY LOVE	129
A HEALTH	130
LONELINESS	131
IN MEMORY OF EUGENE FIELD	133
A SUPPLIANT	134
MOTHERHOOD	135
THE COMMONPLACES	136
JOY ABIDES	137
THE HOURS	138
UNDISMAYED	139
"ALAS! MY OWN HARP!"	140
FAITH	141
BENEATH THE PINES	141
IN LOTUS LAND	142
AN EPITAPH	143
LIFE'S TRINITY	143
FORSAKEN	144
BUD AND BLOOM	144
THE MUSICIAN	145
LOVE AND DEATH	145

Contents.

	PAGE
DEATH	146
THE DEAD SINGER	146
THE ANGELUS	147
BIRTH'S MIRACLE	147
TWO PRAYERS	148
AMBITION	148
LOVE	148
THE POET	149
THE MINSTREL'S POWER	149
LIFE	150
TRADITION	150
THE CREATION OF ART	150
GOD'S CHILDREN	151
IN A VOLUME OF POEMS	151
HERO AND SINGER	151
TO-DAY AND TO-MORROW	152
THE DEAD SEER	152
ONE SAYING	152
TO A SINGER I NEVER SAW	153
LIMITED	153
TRUTH'S MIGHTINESS	153
SELF-MADE	153
THE DEAD WAIF	154
A PRAYER	154
DUTY	154

IN DIALECT.

THE FAITH CURE	157
OLE JIM HANKINS	169
THE BANKS OF TURKEY RUN	177
MORALIZIN'S	184
"'FORE WILLYUM WRIT A BOOK"	187
"WHEN THE ROAS'IN'-EARS IS PLENTY"	189
"PUT 'ER THAYRE FER NINETY DAYS!"	192
AT FWEDDIE'S	194
L'ENVOI	196

THE SOUTHWEST COUNTRY.

STUPENDOUS reach of vale and mountain-side,
   Of wooded continents and seas of plain,
Of grassy oceans glad with isles of grain,
Where trains of traffic, ships of commerce, ride ;
Far distances that rouse prodigious pride
   And clamor hope to hosts that strive in vain,—
   Productive empires boundless, whose rich gain
Shall crown with plenteousness the nations wide !

Thou hast achieved already ! Thy frontiers
   Are mighty with the holy labors wrought
     By nameless heroes of exalted quest ;
And in thy bosom sleep the pioneers
   Who thrilled thy silences with sudden thought
     And woke the vastness of the great southwest !

Songs from the Southwest Country.

THE OPENING OF OKLAHOMA.

APRIL 22, 1889.

At Morning,—The Desert Land.

IN silence, lone and tenantless but fair,
   The desert stands, as on the morn it stood
When God first breathed upon the brooding earth,
And all the throbbing life of wood and field,
Of rounded hills and valleys wide, appeared
In shades and shapes of beauty ; when fond hands
With sweet adornment glorified the world,
Sowed blossoms o'er the gaping mountain-sides,
And wreathed the vales with gladness, while the
   streams
Flowed with bright waters that in music sang
Over the gentle ripples. Perfect world !
New from its Maker's hands, it mutely stood,
Expectant, ready, for its master, Man ;
So stands the desert now, unvexed, unmarred,
By man's relentless labor, sweet and fair

As when God looked upon the new-born earth,
Beheld its perfect comeliness, and said,
" Lo, all is good ! "
                    The grasses waving bend
Before the dewy breezes ; willows nod
Beside the scanty streams, and scattered woods
Breathe sighs of longing welcome ; the wild birds,
Croaking wild cries instinct with fear's alarm,
Shriek out exultant curses ; the fierce beasts,
Bloody from battle with their fellows, go
With haste unwonted to their savage lairs ;
But Nature rules, an empress on whose realm
No foreign footstep falls in rebeldom.
No lazy smoke from chimneys made with hands
Floats in the air ; no human voices vex
The hills and valleys ; no rude labors mar
The swarded prairies' velvet lawns of peace ;
No laughter light, no anguished chorus, floats
From aught save Nature and her savage slaves,
While through the moanings of their restless dreams
There comes no warning of impending change,
Of empire's mighty march ; and man with feet
Shod with the steel of progress fleet and swift,
Beneath whose tread the wilderness shall change,
And at the echoes of whose coming, toil
Shall wake the ages from their solemn sleep,
Order to chaos yield her kingdoms large,
That order may a grander kingdom gain—
And man shall plant his banners flaunting far
With civilization and her thousand arts
That lead and lift the nations to the sky.

At Noon,—The Race for Homes.

Behold ! As from the shades of night
An army gathers full of might,
And strong with constant courage stands
'Tween civilized and savage lands,
Where, vast in power, the legion waits
The turning of the desert gates,
That men of might may enter in
And labor all her glories win !
Lo, where these thousands make assail,
The barren ages all shall fail,
And swift advancement far be hurled
O'er sleeping empires and the world !

The morning hours haste hurried by ;
The noon,—the noon is drawing nigh !
The anxious host with restless eyes
Marks well each rapid hour that flies,
While hope, exulting, wildly rolls
The highest, such as filled the souls
Of Jason and his comrades bold
Who sought the famous fleece of gold,
And bound in one adventurous band
Brought treasures from a foreign land.
Impatient steeds with fretting feet
Upon the trampled grasses beat ;
The dins of harsh, discordant cries
Above the thrilling thousands rise ;
Shrilly the scattered children call,
And soft the words of women fall,

While men with voices hushed and weak
Their low commands impatient speak ;
Till suddenly a mighty cry,
A shout of warning, smites the sky :

"Attention !   Ho,
    Attention here !
   Attention !   Lo,
       The noon is near !"
O'er hill and brake
    Resounds the warning cry ;
    The moment great is nigh ;
   The hosts awake ;
Awake, to strive with mad delight,
Awake, to win the friendly fight !
And from the camps anear and far,
Where nervous haste and hurry are,
Vast legions gather on the plain,
Till chaos and confusion reign ;
The neighing steed with quickened pace
Impatient seeks the vantage-place ;
The slower ox with lightened load
Stands waiting in the crowded road,
And wagon, buggy, carriage, cart,
Vehicles formed with rudest art,
All forward, forward, forward dart,
Swift-forming on the level ground
Where most advantage may be found.

"Line up !   Ho, there !
    Line up !   Line up !"

The Opening of Oklahoma.

The hurried order smites the air;
Above the silent prairies fair
   Unseen progression holds her cup,
Filled to the brim with magic seeds
That harvests hold for human needs.
Excitement grows on beasts and men;
   The saddle-girths are tightened o'er,
   The stirrups lengthened out once more,
And silence softly falls again;
Each bit and buckle, strap and band,
Is tested o'er with careful hand,
Till man and beast, in chosen place,
Stand ready for the coming race.

     The circling sun
His morning race has fully run;
     A waving hand
Signals above the brief command
That sight and sense will understand,—
And open swings the desert land!
A shot! A hundred, thousand more
The grassy meadows echo o'er;
A shout! From countless throats a shout
On rolling wings leaps madly out!
A yell, a raging roar, that flies
   On bounding winds o'er hill and glen,
And 'round the land electrifies
   A thousand living miles of men!

     A mammoth stir,
       A sudden dash,

Swift whip and spur
Together clash,
And wheels on wheels that totter, crash!
They're off! They're off!
Away! Away!
In mad array!
No stop nor stay!
The hurried charge they ride to-day
Would shame and scoff
The Tartar, Turk, and Romanoff!
The race is on;
The host is gone;
All forward thrust
Through clouds of dust;
The thronging legions madly ride
O'er hill and dale,
With hurried pace unsatisfied,
In fierce assail
Where none may fail;
And one by one, exhausted sheer,
The racing thousands disappear;
Till only shadows dimly blent
Tell where the mounted armies went,
Like shifting shadows, faint and dim,
Or ghostly spectres, gaunt and grim,
Beyond the far horizon's rim!

Behold! Adown the valleys bright
The last lone straggler fades from sight,
And only hasty hoof-beats say,
  In echoes from the far-off hills,

What thousands rode the race to-day
  With hopeful hearts and fearless wills;
What hosts with hands that build and bless
Found homes amid the wilderness!

At Night,—The Desert Conquered.

Ten thousand tents above the wilderness,
Conquered so quickly from the lonely realms
And brought beneath man's sceptre of control,
To tremble at his feet and slowly change
Before the forming touches of his hand,
Mark cities newly born, that swift shall grow
The wonders of an age all wonderful.
Ten thousand camp-fires in the valleys broad,
Bright torches of the newer life, whose fires
Advancement's magic hands have widely built,
Show where new homes are founded, and the strife
Which man and nature shall forever wage
Hath here beginning; transformation throws
Her kindly sceptre o'er the lonely lands.
The virgin grasses thrill beneath the tread
Of hurried feet; the wild birds hiding flee,
And savage beasts to savage haunts retire.
Secluded springs, untouched by human lips,
Unvexed by human shadows, since the morn
When first they flowed from earth's abundant breast,
Mirror unwonted faces, fondly press
Soft touches to the unfamiliar lips.
In night's dear arms of rest the wearied hosts
Fall on the conquered fields like warriors old

And dream of homes wrought from the wilderness ;
Of porches wide with clustered blossoms wreathed,
Of lasting shades and tender breezes cool,
Love's gentle looks, and songs of happy birds,
Plenty and progress in a land of might
Rich in the boundless wealth that blesses man
And leads his longings forward to the tall
Results of time and toil's unfailing growth.
Empires arise of pride and promise full,
With conquest high, like prince and peasant won
On fields historic where the clash of arms,
The battle's thunder, and the striving host,
Shook earth's foundations through the lowest depths
And filled the farthest ages with their might.
Dreams fill with wondrous fancies far-off days,
The hills and valleys that with sudden homes
Man's tireless hands have clothed ; but prophecy
Inspires the tender dreams, and time shall fill
Out to the utmost all that fancy forms,
All that she brings from shadows and beholds,
Brighter and greater than the dreams she dreamed.
The world shall search the years' vast volumes o'er
With eagerness and, wearied, rest in vain,
To find another scene for precedent.

THE BALLAD OF THE ALAMO.

O, IT'S East and West and North and South,
—it's the Old World and the New;—
It's every place that the human race has warred and
    wandered through;
But not the years that the ancients lived, nor the years
    that the moderns know,
Such deeds have wrought as the men who fought at
    the Church of the Alamo!

"What see you, frightened sentinel, that thus you
    bend your eyes?
Do herds of cattle or packs of wolves o'erwhelm
    you with surprise?"
"'T is neither wolves nor cattle that march and
    march again;
"'T is Santa Anna's army,—'t is twice three thou-
    sand men!"

"Nay, nay, my faithful guardsman!—God's curses
    on the foe!—
You must be mad or drunken,—your eyes deceive
    you so!

For Santa Anna's far away with all his blare and
 boast,
Afraid to battle freedom's few with his unnum-
 bered host!"

"'T is he,—the Greaser! he, I know! There—
 yonder—in the west!
Mine eyes do not deceive me,—no! His lances are
 at rest;
The long lines sweep and forward creep, beneath
 the gleaming sun!
O God of Freedom, help us now! They're fifty
 to our one!"

"Ho, troopers, to your saddles now! You—you!
 Ride—ride—your best!
To where yon guardsman says he sees the
 Greasers in the west;
Right bold ye are! Ride fast and far! And,
 prove it ill or well,
Bring back report! We'll make work short with
 these wild imps of hell!"

Forth, forth they ride; up yon hillside, with hoofs
 that spurn the ground,
The horses gallop, gallop on, with faint and fainter
 sound;
And o'er the summit, passing down, the horsemen
 slowly sink,
With courage whirled into that world which waits
 beyond the brink.

"A musket-shot? A pistol-shot? Ride, ride, ride,
  men, for life!
A hundred lancers after them! God! for an equal
  strife!
Fling wide the gates! There safety waits for all who
  love the Star;
And Death's red wounds to all that dare with it to
  offer war!

"And yonder comes the armied host! Ah, guard,
  your eyes were true!
And yonder comes the horse and foot that shall
  make short of you!
Short shift of you, short shift of us,—they're fifty
  to our one!
The battle would be over here before the fight
  begun!

"The Church! The Church! Its courts are wide,
  its walls are firm and strong!"
O'er Brazos' stream, with herd and team, the heroes
  move along;
They are not first, they are not last, of those who
  from the foe
Found refuge sure and safe, secure, within the
  Alamo!

Now pause, ye foes! Your leader well the strength
  and power has known
Of hearts and souls aflame for right and for
  their country's own!

Beyond your arms, despising harms, triumphant over ills,
They'll meet attack and hurl you back, while every bullet kills!

"A messenger! A Flag of Truce! What does the Wolf presume?
Thinks he that we'll surrender now? Too well we know that doom!
But ride you forth and meet him there, and bring his word to me:
A cannon-shot from hell red-hot my sole reply shall be!

"The Greaser Dog! 'Surrender at discretion; with a word,
If you persist in holding out, your hearts shall have the sword!'
Ho, gunner, pull the lanyard now! A throat of flame shall show
How such commands from despot lips receive the answer 'No!'

"Now look you, comrade soldiers! On San Fernando's towers
A blood-red rag supplants the Flag! No quarter shall be ours!
But his the blood whose coward flood shall run the valleys through!
Now 'God and Texas' be our cry for God and Texas, too!"

The foe draws nigh; and thundering high wild
    roars the cannonade;
And yonder o'er the rolling stream a hasty bridge
    is made;
But the rifles of the Texans are aimed at heart and
    head,
And like the leaves in autumn-time the Mexicans
    are dead!

Loud ring the cries of conflict! Loud roll and roar
    the guns,
And nearer, nearer, creep the lines to Freedom's
    watching sons;
Each single night with deadly might the batteries
    leap and glow,
While every road is garrisoned with thousands of
    the foe.

"Thrice welcome, men from Gonzales! Thrice wel-
    come, one and all!
You've hurried far and here you are, and here we'll
    fight and fall;
You'll find some neat diversion sweet before you
    leave, my braves,
But arms all true of thirty-two are worth a thousand
    slaves!"

Now yonder on the eastern road the skirmished
    horsemen fight;
Now yonder by the river-side the jackals flame at
    night;

But closer draw the batteries,—the Wolf will have
   his own!
Send, send for help, brave Travis! You are too
   weak alone!

" Now saddle up your swiftest horse, and draw the
   cinches tight,—
It is a wild and lonely ride that you must make
   to-night!
Away to Houston at the front, and tell him that we
   call
For men to help and men to hope and men to save
   us all!

" And should relief not come to us,—we never shall
   retreat!
Our flag shall float,—we will not yield,—to die for
   home is sweet!
Like soldiers who can ne'er forget love to their land
   is due,—
We all shall live with honor still, and die with honor
   too!

" And hasten, Bonham, hasten, on steeds that gallop
   mad!
Away, away! No stop nor stay! Away to Goliad!
For Fannin with his strong right arm and his three
   hundred men
Shall overthrow the Greaser foe and scourge him
   home again!"

Then Travis called his men to him: "The end is
　　near," said he;
"But yet there's room to slip the doom, for all who
　　care to flee!
As for myself, here shall I stay, whatever fate may
　　chance:
Let him who wills to share my ills across this line
　　advance!"

Then down he stooped and drew his sword, and on
　　the trampled sod
He traced a line of straight design: "For Texas
　　and our God,"
In grim prayer rose from lips of those, and up he
　　glanced, to find
Eight score and more had stepped it o'er, and none
　　were left behind!

There are men and women that perish; they die on the
　　sea and the shore,
For the storm and the plague and the bullet are awake
　　and at work evermore;
But the angels above who are watching sing gladly
　　with glorified breath
When the men who may choose base living refuse and
　　go bravely down to the death!

　　　*　　*　　*　　*　　*　　*

Be ready, O ye heroes, by despot arms assailed!
For Houston is at Washington and Fannin's men
　　have failed;

Your eyes are tired with watching, your hope and
 help are gone,
And Santa Anna's savage hosts will storm the fort
 at dawn!

The bugles blare the frenzied "Charge!" The
 bands Deguelo play;
The cry, "No quarter," leaps and rolls above the
 morning gray;
Now God protect the heroes there! If Santa Anna
 wins,
Each Texan there shall slaughter share, if once the
 work begins.

In yonder plaza stands the chief beside the hidden
 gun,
While forward, forward, in attack the footmen rush
 and run;
To north and east, to north and west, the thronging
 thousands swarm,
And oh, the horrid wings of death that ride upon
 the storm!

On still they sweep! Is there no help—no arm
 outstretched to save?
Alas, that might can conquer right, the many slay
 the brave!
Like shambled sheep the thousands leap across the
 wall,—and—then—
From room to room—they drive—to—doom—the
 still unconquered men!

Here Travis fell; here Bonham died; here Evans
 perished, too;
There Crockett fell, by danger slain, who danger
 never knew;
There Bowie, on his bed of death, with pistols made
 reply
To all his foes required of him, and taught them
 how to die!

How red and rare the deep wounds stare! The
 Church this Sabbath day
Knows scenes that none e'er saw before who
 gathered here to pray;
For dead and dying Mexicans are counted hundreds
 five,
And of the gallant Texans not one is left alive!

God rest them well! Their blood and brawn were
 gifts to liberty;
They died to save the Lone Star Flag, and make
 their people free;
And love shall keep their holy sleep and twine
 sweet garlands when
The heart of Freedom mourns above brave Travis
 and his men.

*O, it's East and West and North and South,—it's the
 Old World and the New;
It's every place that the human race has warred and
 wandered through;*

*But not the years that the ancients lived nor the years
    that the moderns know
Such deeds have wrought as the men who fought at the
    Church of the Alamo!*

THE BATTLE OF THE WASHITA.

(The battle of the Washita was fought November 28, 1868, near the present town of Cheyenne, Roger Mills County, Oklahoma, between General Custer's Seventh Cavalry and Black Kettle's band of Indians.)

THERE are battles by populous cities and battles where business roars ;
There are battles in song-famous valleys and battles on ballad-sung shores ;
But the battles that conquered the prairies and laid the red devils to rest
Are the battles of bounty and blessing that live in the lives of the West.

There's many a soldier lives in song whose deathless deeds were bold,
But Custer was much the bravest man that ever had heart of gold ;
There's many a regiment rolled in fame, but none could braver be
Than the men who rode to the Washita in the Seventh Cavalry !

The savage tribes in paint and plume have danced the dance of war,
And bursting from the far southwest have wandered fast and far ;

And where they sweep the settler's keep in fire and
    smoke has fled,
While settler, wife, and children,—all are lying
    scalped and dead!

The swart Cheyenne and Kiowa, the tall Arapahoe,
Comanche, and Apache fierce, have joined the
    fiendish foe;
And swift along the far frontier with fire and slaugh-
    ter, too,
They 've scourged the Kansas hills and plains with
    deeds that demons do.

" Ho, to your saddles, Custer! " Then thundered
    Sheridan;
" There 's work to do for such as you and for your
    gallant men;
I trust you well in everything; with neither wait
    nor word
Drive back these beasts into their lairs and make
    them feel your sword! "

" My boys are quick and tireless, sir; no blade of
    grass shall grow
Beneath our feet until we meet and slay the savage
    foe;
With lively pains we 'll scour the plains; we 'll
    soothe to rest again
The seven seas of broad prairies and give them back
    to men! "

"Now, red-skins, to your villages, and pray the
    Manitou,
For Custer and his cavalry are on the trail for you!
And you shall feel their swords of steel,—'t is war's
    relentless law,—
And see your lodges stained with blood beside the
    Washita."

It was a gallant regiment that marched from old
    Fort Hays
To hunt the prowling savages in those October
    days;
High beat their hearts and fearless, and plagues of
    want and woe
Were bred to fall on each and all that dared to be
    a foe!

It 's southward over Kansas the eager troopers
    press;
It 's past Fort Dodge, and on and on, into the wil-
    derness;
It 's marching, marching, through the day, it 's
    mounting guard by night,
Until at last the game is treed; now, soldiers, to the
    fight!

"Ho, troopers, do you see it? Here runs the re-
    cent trail!
Not far the Indian village now; your mission shall
    not fail;

Ere long the murdered white men, the women worse
    than slain,
By your brave arms avenge their harms, and rest at
    peace again."

Through sleet and snow the soldiers go ; what mat-
    ters wind or cold ?
Their strong hearts warm defy the storm, with cour-
    age brave and bold ;
Though quick-sands yawn and ice impedes, yet
    uncomplainingly
They forward march where Custer leads — the
    Seventh Cavalry !

" Now steadily and silently, O scouts, with caution
    crawl !
A single sound may reach the foe, and warn him
    once for all ;
Too far we come, too far we march ; 't were ever-
    more our shame,
If some neglect should rouse him now, and rob us
    us of our game.

" Ho, ho ! Ho, ho ! Here ashes glow ! We now
    are near at last ;
Heard ye that howl ? A snapping cur growls o'er
    his rough repast !
And — lower still ! Ye gods, what ill ! A baby's
    fretful cry !
Alas, that men such deeds must do, and little ones
    must die ! "

Now to the east and to the west and to the north and south,
The men in silence find their way across the valley's mouth;
O sleeping red-skins, to your prayers! Invoke the Manitou,
For Custer and his cavalry are all surrounding you!

It's little rest the soldiers take; it's little sleep they know,
So cold the night howls overhead, so deep the drifted snow;
But tired limbs and heavy eyes have hastened far away,
For " Garryowen " and the " Charge " shall sound at break of day.

" The East grows pale; the shadows fail! When will the bugle blow?
Whose that command which lags behind,—which keeps us waiting so?"
Hark! Loud and clear with cheer on cheer the " Charge " rings on the air,
And, ere the lodges leap awake, the strong-limbed men are there!

Now steady, steady, steady, men! Be cautious through the strife!
Each lodge leaps up, the village wakes, with savage, naked life!

On fast and far! On, lines of war! Like tigers
    for their prey,
Sweep onward still o'er highest hill, and every foe-
    man slay!

But yonder, yonder fires the foe from every far
    ravine!
And yonder, yonder, through the trees, the skulk-
    ing braves are seen!
And there, and here, from tepees near, the swarthy
    squaws reveal
With deadly rifles aimed too well, the deadly hate
    they feel!

Let not that dirge wake pity now! Hard, hard let
    hearts remain!
So shrieked, so mourned white women, too, o'er
    babes and husbands slain!
'T is but the death-song born of fear; if Death is
    master there,
God let them know how fierce is woe that prays a
    hopeless prayer!

Behind each bush a foeman lurks—behind each rock
    and tree;
Charge right and left! Charge back and forth, till
    every one shall flee!
Red hearts must feel the stroke of steel; for still
    their victims cry
For vengeance on the ruthless foe,—for vengeance
    mountains high!

Up hill, down vale, the troopers charge; and fast
    the warriors all
Before the swords of righteous wrath in terror flee
    and fall;
And every stroke writes down in blood what ne'er
    was writ before,
"Black Kettle and his savage band shall ride the
    plains no more!"

Now rest ye, gallant troopers all! The weary chase
    is done;
The savages are loose no more, the battle has been
    won;
These ghastly forms—five score and more—pro-
    claim how well have wrought
Your soldier arms, your soldier swords, that leaped
    with righteous thought.

O sleepers on the wide, wide plains! O mangled,
    murdered men!
Not unavenged you rest to-day for all you suffered
    then!
Your savage foes are silent now; these stains upon
    the snow
Are red as those beside your doors a few short weeks
    ago!

    *   *   *   *   *   *   *

Where thus the white and red man strove, some
    thirty years ago,
The stains no more make red the soil, and greenest
    grasses grow;

And happy homes where roses twine and children
  laugh and play
Have filled with peace the vast frontiers since that
  eventful day.

No more the war-paint redly glows upon the war-
  rior's face;
No more the war-dance reels and roars through all
  a savage race;
No more the bands of mounted braves in haste and
  hurry ride
To murder men and ply the torch, through all the
  borders wide.

No more red hands and redder hearts have king-
  doms for their reigns;
No more the war-whoops roll and ring across the
  desert plains;
No more the war-drums send abroad their doleful
  melody,
Since Custer led his gallant men,—the Seventh
  Cavalry!

*There are battles by populous cities and battles where
  business roars;
There are battles in song-famous valleys and battles
  on ballad-sung shores;
But the battles that conquered the prairies and laid the
  red devils to rest
Are the battles of bounty and blessing that live in the
  lives of the West!*

THE PLAINT OF THE TENDERFOOT.

DOWN along the Cimarron where the currents twine,
There I met an immigrant in eighteen eighty-nine;
He was all alone and his heart was stone,—he had gathered bitter fruit,
And his hoarse voice rang as he sadly sang the Plaint of the Tenderfoot:

From Indiana it was I came, some seventeen days ago,
To find me a farm in the "Beautiful Land" that the boomers have tried to blow;
And in those few days I have lived more ways than the brutes of the jungles do;
I have seen more things than a bird with wings could flutter or fly up through;
And if ever I do get home again, though bacon and bread be slack,
I'll be content with a bit of both, and a clean shirt to my back.

I have learned some things that are valuable; it is now quite plain to me
This opening up new lands to the world isn't what it is said to be;

With the "sooner" before and the "sooner" behind,
   the honest man has no chance ;
They 'll gobble his claim and blacken his name and
   take every cent in his pants :
And if ever I do get home again, no matter how
   much I lack,
I 'll be content with an empty purse, and a clean
   shirt to my back.

I stopped at Arkansas City, and bought me a horse
   and cart ;
I crossed the Strip in elegant style, with a high and
   hopeful heart ;
And "overland fish" was all my grub, and my drink
   was the water white
Which rose in the tracks that the cattle made,
   through the dews of the chilly night ;
And if ever I do get home again, they may call me
   white or black,
But I 'll be content with an oat-straw bed, and a
   clean shirt to my back.

I travelled a hundred miles, I think, and I slept on
   the ground, I know ;
I never have washed or shaved my face since fifteen
   days ago ;
For the wild wolves howled and ran them round in
   the most alarming curves,
And I am not used to that sort of thing,—it is wear-
   ing on my nerves !

And if ever I do get home again, I may fall into
    wrong and rack,
But I'll be content with a quiet place, and a clean
    shirt to my back.

I ran a race for a dozen miles,—a wild and a reck-
    less race,—
That far surpassed Dick Turpin's ride or a London
    steeple-chase ;
And when I stopped, not a single soul,—not a thing
    was there in sight,—
But a vast amount of the meanest land that ever
    lay out at night ;
And if ever I do get home again, I'll stay in the
    beaten track,
And be content with a good clean face, and a clean
    shirt to my back.

But in half an hour on that very claim there were
    six men holding it,
(I never hold out for a swine myself and I know
    when it's time to quit ;)
So I sold my right for a paltry five, and had given
    the buyer ten
To take the quarter and let me go and live in the
    world again ;
And if ever I do get home again, no matter how
    small my pack,
I'll be content with a good whole skin, and a clean
    shirt to my back.

I never was used to rifles much and pistols take my sand,
And the boomers that love this soil so much have one or the other at hand ;
And grub's too dear for a man out here, and if I should the State receive,
I never would stay but would up and away, as soon as I ever could leave ;
And if ever I do get home again, I'll sail on a safer tack,
And be content with the breath of life, and a clean shirt to my back.

I've driven that horse on water and grass some thousands of miles, I know ;
I've shivered with cold and thirsted for drink and famished for eatables so !
But you never can see what a fool you can be till you turn yourself over and try,
And you cannot be sure what a broncho 'll endure from the pauper-born look of his eye ;
And if ever I do get home again, then death to the boomer's clack !
For I'll be content with my hair slicked up, and a clean shirt to my back.

Here's the horse and cart and the love of my heart to whoever will ship me home ;
Should I live as long as Methuselah did, I never again will roam ;

I'll return elate to the Hoosier State,—it is far too good for me!
This opening up new lands to the world isn't what it is said to be;
And if ever I do get home again, I'll stay till the earth shall crack,
And be content with a six-foot-two, and a clean shirt to my back!

Down along the Cimarron, where the currents twine,
There I met an immigrant in eighteen eighty-nine;
He was all alone and his heart was stone,—he had gathered bitter fruit,
And his hoarse voice rang as he sadly sang this Plaint of the Tenderfoot!

SLAUGHTERING THE PONIES.

(After the battle of the Washita, eight hundred Indian ponies, which had been captured, were shot under General Custer's order, to prevent their re-capture by the Indians from whom they had been taken.)

Battle is Battle and War is War ;
Soldiers must do what their swords abhor ;
And he who wins in the fierce assails
Suffers and sins, like the one who fails.

" Round up the horses, troopers ; we march at early dawn ;
Round up the horses quickly,—the forage all is gone ;
And take the Indian ponies,—eight hundred, so you say,—
And shoot them in the valley about the break of day."

The battle all is over ; the warriors far have fled,
Save something like a hundred braves that slumber stark and dead ;
The captured squaw and papoose are under guard, to be
The trophies of the victors,—the Seventh Cavalry.

Slaughtering the Ponies.

It is a hundred miles or more ere they can reach again
The quarters full of forage for jaded beasts and men;
The savages are everywhere; a few short hours, and they
Will ambush all the narrow trails and challenge to the fray.

The captives must be guarded, too, and all must march in haste;
With famine fourteen hours ahead, there is no time to waste;
'T were folly deep the spoils to keep while facing such a foe,
For, thus encumbered, all would die, while marching through the snow.

"Round up the horses, troopers; the forage all is gone;
And, sergeant, take the ponies and slaughter them at dawn;
Eight hundred Indian ponies once dead, and we shall find
Our enemies dismounted a hundred miles behind!"

*   *   *   *   *   *

The bugle wakes the sleepers; the east is purple quite,
And "Boots and Saddles" rouses the camp at morning light;

'T is time that all were moving; the rations are so small
The soldiers and the captives can hardly eat at all.

It's back to Old Cantonment they go with horse and men;
It's back to hear the praises of warlike Sheridan;
It's back from all their hardships, with rest and victory
Upon the famous banners of the Seventh Cavalry!

"Forward!" the order echoes; and forward up the hill,
The soldiers and their captives move swiftly with a will;
For well the weary troopers with eager longings know
That cozy barracks warm and snug are just across the snow.

They march in silence forward; hark! Through the valley runs
The rolling roar of firing from half a hundred guns;
The horses leap in terror; a soldier mutters low,
"They're killing off the ponies we captured from the foe!"

Yet fainter grows the firing, and fainter, fainter still,
Till single shots alone are heard across the wooded hill;

Then silence falls behind them, and all the troopers
  know
Eight hundred Indian ponies are dead upon the
  snow!

Upon a swinging gallop the troop belated comes
And joins the marching columns, but silent are the
  drums;
And as they swing in squadron each trooper's eyes
  are dim,
Because some helpless pony received a shot from
  him!

Excusable? Assuredly! No censure dare befall!
To win excuses everything; 'tis failing blames it
  all!
They won; they won it bravely; who dares to
  question aught
Of all the mighty deeds they did, when once the
  deeds are wrought?

These piles of bones, you ask me? These piles of
  bones they made
That cold November morning at War's heroic trade,
When Custer slaughtered quickly here in the
  drifted snow
Eight hundred Indian ponies, some thirty years ago!

>*Battle is Battle and War is War;*
>*Soldiers must do what their swords abhor;*
>*And he who wins in the fierce assails*
>*Suffers and sins, like the one who fails!*

DAVID L. PAYNE.

'TIS he that finds
New hopes for human grieving,
New homes for men and women, who is great;
He frees their minds,
He conquers their bereaving,
And leads them forth,—the builders of the state.

Not he that fills
The world with blood and battle
Is most the hero, though he win a crown;
The brute that kills
Is worse than brutal cattle
That blindly crush their weaker fellows down.

Though wars may rage,
In bread, not blood, is glory,—
The plow is more exalted than the sword;
Who tells his age
Advancement's mighty story
Thrills all the future with each potent word.

And such was Payne:
His country's battles over,
He stormed the desert,—bade the thousands come;

Of wood and plain
He made himself a rover,
Homeless to win the homeless hosts a home.

A new Crusade
He preached, a second Hermit,
A savage land from wildness to redeem;
He slowly made,
Whatever fools may term it,
A mighty force that realized his dream.

He first conceived
A homeless people making
Glad homes of plenty where the coyotes ran;
He first believed
This hidden land, forsaking
Its desert ways, would leap the thrones of man.

He broke no law,
And yet the law's defenders
Upon his guiltless head their vengeance poured;
The lion's paw
That only helpless renders
Tossed him, poor victim, and the lion roared!

And foolish men,
Both civilized and savage,
Swore he was wrong, and cursed with venom white;
They called him then
An outlaw, born for ravage,
A bandit chief, and locked him from the light.

The soldiers came
And led him forth in fetters,—
A free man chained in Freedom's nooning time ;
The prison shame,
The dungeon damp, in letters
Burning with blackness, branded him with crime.

Yet forth he walked,
Defying force and faction,
A martyr scourged and beaten for his cause ;
And as he talked,
Demanding onward action,
He shamed the people for their shameful laws.

His ardent hopes,
Like some divine aroma,
Pervaded all the globe with sweet perfume ;
And o'er the slopes
Advanced young Oklahoma,
His child of light, to make the desert bloom.

This be his fame :
The prison cell defying,
He led mankind where bayonets blocked the way ;
So shall his name
In hearts of love undying
Live through the ages to the farthest day.

For those that lead,
Despising death and danger,
The ages build Fame's restless telegraph ;

He led, indeed ;
And for the careless stranger
Who knew him not, this be his epitaph :

He dreamed and wrought,
And dreaming wrought unceasing
To shape his dreams and fill them to the full ;
He dreamed and thought
Of mighty States increasing,
And gave his life to make them possible!

KANSAS.

SHE felt, they say,
The battle-storms of earth,
The cannons cradled her,
The war-drums beat fierce lullabies
At her wild birth ;
Yet she in danger found a paradise,
And bowed,—its worshipper !

'T was thus she roused
The multitudes to arms,
And made the nations feel
The precepts they had taught and talked
Of hurts and harms ;
Until God came and led her, and she walked
The child of sword and steel.

What though she loves
The Novel and the New?
What though she sometimes fall
When scaling heights of sky and star
To find the True?
For him that strives, God's angels shall unbar
The gates of all in all!

What though her wounds
Be many and severe?
What though her shoulder bend
Beneath the crushing loads
She does not fear?
Travel is easy in the beaten roads,—
Ease has no worthy end.

Though bruises come,
The brave pursue the quest;
Though failure and defeat
Their harsh, ignoble measures sing,
To strive is best;
To sloth the Fates no crowns of laurel bring,
And conquering is sweet.

Who never strives
Forever falls and fails
Where Terror sways her hosts
And Force with all the fraud of greeds
Makes fierce assails;
"T is only he that battles on and bleeds
Deserves his boasts.

She seeks the New,—
She loves its laughing youth;
She leaves the Old, as fear
Forsakes the ways of pestilence;
And for the truth,
Warm in the heart of high Omnipotence,
She struggles year by year.

Her heart, her hope,
Is boundless as her plains;
She walks the starry ways,
She leaps the vale and mountain-side,
For endless gains;
Her faith haunts all the far horizons wide
With voice of prayer and praise!

And so to thee,
O Kansas, unto thee,
Proud child of tale and song,
Whom brave men filled with hope and health,
Let blessings be!
Thou hast the soul of empires, commonwealth
Whose infancy was strong!

Free blood fast bounds
Along the sleepy veins
At mention of thy name;
Thine eyes are on the future, great
With wondrous gains;
Such be thy glory, and the years elate
Shall justify thy fame!

THE STAMPEDE.

WE took our turn at the guard that night, just
    Sour-dough Charlie and I,
And as we mounted our ponies, there were clouds
    in the western sky;
And we knew that before the morning the storm by
    the north wind stirred
Would scourge the plains with its furies fierce and
    madden the savage herd;
But we did not shrink the danger; we had ridden
    the plains for years,—
The crash of the storm and the cattle's cry were
    music in our ears.

We drove the herd to a circle; for the winds were
    calm, and we knew
That somewhere near to the midnight shift the
    storm-fiends would be due;
We rode the rounds unceasingly, and we worked
    with an anxious will
Until the cattle were lying down and the mighty
    herd was still,
And only the musical breathing of the bedded
    beasts arose
As we rounded the living circle and guarded their
    light repose.

Then the storm came on in anger; the winds of a
    sudden turned,
The lightnings flamed through the seething skies,
    and the prairies blazed and burned ;
The thunders rolled like an avalanche, and they
    shook the rocking world,
That trembling quaked as the storm so wild its ban-
    ners of blaze unfurled ;
The fires flew over the frightened herd and leaped
    from horn to horn
Till horrible clamors rose and fell in chaos of fear
    forlorn.

The herd awoke in a minute ; but we rode through
    the flashing ways
And sang with a will the olden songs we learned in
    our childhood days ;
The human voice has a wondrous power, and the
    wildest beast that moans
Forgets its fear in a dream of peace at the sound of
    its tender tones ;
And on through the blinding flashes and on through
    the dark and the light,
We rode with the old songs ringing, and we prayed
    for the death of night.

I never could tell how it happened; there came a
    tremendous crash,
A wolf jumped out of the chaparral,—and the herd
    was off in a flash !
And Charlie was riding before them ; then I saw
    him draw his gun

And fire at the plunging leaders, till he turned them
    one by one ;
Then the darkness fell,—I could not see,—and then
    in the blinding light
My pard went down, and the maddened herd swept
    on through the savage night !

Him I found where the cattle rushed in the wild of
    their wandering,
Broken and beaten by scores of hoofs, a crushed and
    a mangled thing !
And his pony lay with a broken leg, as dead as a
    rotten log,
Where its foot had slipped in the hidden hole of a
    worthless prairie-dog.
We buried him there—you can see the stones—and
    whether we die or live,
We gave him the best of a funeral that a cowboy
    camp can give.

His name ? It was Sour-dough Charlie, sir ; and
    whether a good or bad,
We called him that for a score of years—it was all
    the name he had !
I found a locket above his heart, with a picture
    there of grace
That showed a girl with a curly head and a most
    uncommon face ;
Hero, you say ? Well, maybe so ; for I know it is
    oft confessed
That he's the kind of a man it takes for the work
    here in the West.

A SONG FOR THE SETTLER.

THERE are songs for the valiant soldier
    Who fights for his native shore
And carries her dauntless banners
    On a hundred fields or more ;
There are songs for the gallant sailor
    Who conquers the crested foam,—
Then a song for the prairie settler,—
    The man in the dug-out home !

He battles the boundless prairies,
    He sabres the savage soil,
He masters the foes that face him,
    With the might of his tireless toil ;
The plow is the flashing weapon
    That slaughters the sodden loam,
And over them all he triumphs,—
    The man in the dug-out home.

What matters the howling blizzard,
    The hot winds and the heat?
Through summer and winter he marches
    With the tread of victorious feet ;

He turns the sod and he sows it,—
    He reaps, whatever may come,
And Plenty crowns with her blessedness
    The man in the dug-out home.

He toils, and the barren desert,
    Forgetting its former days,
Transforms itself to a garden,
    With a garden's wondrous ways ;
And contentment fills his bosom
    While morning and evening gloam,—
He's a king that owns his kingdom,—
    The man in the dug-out home !

His coming is swift and silent ;
    He carries no sounding drum,
But the savage hosts of the desert flee
    Whenever his legions come ;
He conquers the untamed prairies,
    He masters the stubborn land,
Till towns and cities and commonwealths
    Arise at his regal hand.

O man in the prairie dug-out,
    Your peaceful arts are best,
You have made new homes for the hopes of men,
    You have built the wondrous West ;
And all that it holds exalted,
    And all that it prizes true,
Would never have been without the toil
    Of a hero such as you !

Then a song for the valiant settler,
   And a song for his humble home!
For the valleys laugh and the prairies bloom
   Wherever his feet may roam!
He scatters the countless blessings
   That never their bounties cease,
This man that is more than hero
   In his dug-out home of peace!

LINES ON CAPTAIN PAYNE'S CABIN.

WITHIN this humble cabin dwelt
   A man who mankind's longing felt;
Who bravely strove and proudly wrought
To fill his one heroic thought;
Who, seeking homes for thousands, made
His bold incursions unrepaid,
Though this, his castle, rose to bless
With peace the savage wilderness,
A light that saw, as once did he,
The mighty commonwealths to be.

His was the mind that dared receive
What others only half believe;
His was the heart that knew the need
And dared the homeless hundreds lead;
His were the feet that dared to stand
Undaunted in the savage land;
And his the hands that crowned his plan,
And gave the desert back to man.

These are his meeds : Homes fill the plains
Where he, a martyr, walked in chains,
And every prison where he came
Is holy with his holy fame ;
The vales with towns are thicker set
Than once with sword and bayonet,
And every place where once he stood
Proclaims the glories of his good.

He dared ; he did ; and thus 't is so
He reaps rewards that heroes know :
A name that grateful people crown
With lofty praise and high renown ;
For kindly Heaven to him sent
A commonwealth for monument ;
Undying, unforgotten, then,
While lives a loving race of men !

MOUNTAIN SONG.

AWAY to the mountains, away, away !
    Beyond the desolate plains that rise
From hollow vales where the rivers play,
    To the snowy summits that reach the skies !
The treasures of gold for our coming wait
    Beyond the desert so grim and gray ;
Then a sigh and a tear for the loved ones here,
    And away to the mountains, away, away !

Away to the mountains, away, away!
    Their giant veins with a golden flood
Throb ever, forever, and riot gay
    With regal riches of royal blood;
The odorous pines with their balmy breath
    Shall waft us a welcome, for aye, for aye;
Then a tear and a sigh and a tender good-bye,
    And away to the mountains, away, away!

Away to the mountains, away, away!
    To dig and delve at their heart's rich core,
To cut and carve where the treasures stay,
    And stain our hands with their yellow gore;
And after the moments of toil and care,
    We shall be happy as Spring's bright day;
Then a sigh and a kiss for the ones we shall miss,
    And away to the mountains, away, away!

"WHEN THE GOLDEN-ROD IS YELLOW."

DREAMY haze of languor fills
    All the smoky valleys tender,
And above the haloed hills
    Hangs the Summer's golden splendor;
Fields are rich with ripened grain,
    Orchards bend with fruitage mellow,
Plenty rules the boundless plain,—
    When the golden-rod is yellow.

Spring, so young and debonair,
  Fell before the mighty Summer,
And old Winter, worn with care,
  Overthrows the Autumn comer;
Gladness heaps the hearts of need,
  All are kings and none the fellow,
And the world is bright indeed,
  When the golden-rod is yellow.

Let contentment rule the board,
  Sing the songs that banish sadness;
Nature brings the bounties stored
  When the days were full of gladness;
Happiness shall lift her voice
  When the tempests rage and bellow,
For the sons of men rejoice
  When the golden-rod is yellow.

ON THE SHANKY-TANK.

O THE shady Shanky-tank! There the willows rich and rank
  Bend their happy heads together o'er the water's dimpled face,
And with arms of gladdest glee clasp in royal revelry
  All the winsome, winding river in a rapturous embrace!

Evermore a chorus swells from the tinkle of the bells
  Where the cows a-lowing loiter in the meadows on the bank,

And a boyish whistle throws all the music heaven
    knows
  From the birds that warble ever up and down the
    Shanky-tank.

Days of laughter live again through the yearning
    years of men,
  And I blithely bend unwearied o'er the water
    waves below,
Underneath the sycamore, just as in the hours of
    yore,
  And the fishes bite forever through the vanished
    Long Ago.

Or secure in cool retreat from Midsummer's burning
    heat,
  Poised above the placid waters in the shadows
    deep and dim,
There I plunge with sudden spring, claiming Neptune for my king,
  And, a fondly fearless merman, pass a pleasant
    hour with him.

Oh, my feet unwearied are, though I wander fast and
    far
  Where the angels romped with boyhood through
    each happy quip and prank,
And again my longings dine from the tables spread
    so fine
  With ambrosial foods and nectars on the shady
    Shanky-tank!

OKLAHOMA.

HERE through the ages old the desert slept
    In solitudes unbroken, save when passed
The bison herds, and savage hunters swept
    In thundering chaos down the valleys vast;
But lo! across the desert margins stepped
    Progression's mighty legions, and one blast
    From her transforming trumpet filled the last
Lone covert where affrighted wildness crept.

Full armed and armored at her wondrous birth,
    Her shining temples wreathed with gorgeous dower,
She sits among the empires of the earth;
    Her proud achievements o'er the nations tower,
Won by her people with their royal worth
    Of lofty culture, wisdom, wealth, and power!

THE MISSISSIPPI.

THIS mighty stream that types a people free,
    Upon whose breast the argosies of pride
    And all the navies of the nations ride,
Sings evermore exalted songs to me;
The margins tall breathe hymns of majesty,
    And every eddy of the onward tide,
    An orchestra, quires endless music wide,
And full of peace, and tender as the sea.

A thousand cities by thee burn and blaze,
  Vast commonwealths beside thee sentry keep,
    And empires o'er thee clasp their guarding hands ;
Yet my full heart hears anguish in thy lays :
  Old mountain mem'ries in their dirges weep
    And, in their ditties, sigh for unseen lands !

THE PLAINS.

THEY called them " Deserts " once; but like a sea
    The tides of life with leaping currents warm
  Swept in the countless millions, swarm on swarm,
And covered all their vast immensity ;
The wildness changed to bounties for the free,
    And man's firm hand tamed there the savage storm,
  And slowly sure came rounding into form
The giant limbs of commonwealths to be.

These prairies teem with plenty ; these high streams
  Roll rich, unmeasured lengths of waters down ;
And cities are beside them, whose fair dreams
  With stately splendor every hilltop crown ;
Each valley smiles with gladness, and it seems
  The desert has forgotten how to frown.

BY THE OVERLAND TRAIL.

THIS was the path of empire. Fifty years
    Have hung their halos where heroic rolled
The white-topped wagons of the pioneers
    Who walked the desert ways for dreams of gold.
How gaunt and ghastly spread the far frontiers
    With care and carnage for the pale-face bold,
When savage legions with embattled spears
    Brought death and danger to the days of old !

Here crossed the prairies toward the Golden Gates
    The fathers, founders of the newer West ;
They conquered kingdoms in their mighty quest,
And sowed the seeds of cities, towns, and states ;
    Lo, by their prowess is the present blest,
And on their glory all the future waits !

WHERE CUSTER FELL.

WHERE Custer fell ! The nation strows
    The brightest garlands Honor knows
  Upon the marbles that alway
  Mark holy mounds of yellow clay,
And wreaths of glory there bestows.

The Little Big Horn softly goes
Around the ridges, and it flows
  With sweeter music all the day
      Where Custer fell.

For him, the Matchless, him and those
Who died with him before their foes,
  Let Grandeur twine her laurels gay,
  Let Freedom shout their fame and say:
" Heroes of might alone repose
      Where Custer fell!"

THE COWBOY POET.

O'ER the prairies vast of created things roam
    the steers of my thoughts in herds,
Where I round them up for the branding-iron and I
    lariat them with words;
Then away to the great corrals of books do I drive
    the unruly throng,
Till the world appears at the stock-yard pens and
    receives them there in song!

THE SUNFLOWER.

IN pomp this princess of the prairie stands,
    A crown of gold upon her head sublime;
She sways her sceptre o'er the gorgeous lands
    And rules, the mistress of the realms of time;
But from her eyes no glances earthward run:
She gazing worships toward her god, the sun!

SONNETS.

BOOKS.

THESE are not ink and paper! They are souls
    That strove in travail; they are lives of tears;
The brain-throbs and the heart-beats of long
    years
Writhe in dumb agony upon these scrolls!
Here smiles the Hope that like an ocean rolls
    From Deed to Duty; here weep doubts and fears
    In bosoms tremulous; here Love endears
Disconsolate toil and endless hate controls.

Aye, these are inspiration! In the low
    Sad hours of weakness, they are stores of might;
They treasure truths eternal, and they glow
    With stars brought earthward from unmeasured
        Night;
Somewhat of God's great verities they know,
    Somewhat of Man's far future and its light!

THE TEACHER.

BEHOLD the Priest of Knowledge! On the
    heights
    Where vast Omniscience over-arching broods,
    He stands with Truth, in whose infinitudes
Blaze the swung censers and the altar lights;

There he, beloved of Wisdom and her rites,
   Receives the verities and endless goods,
   The graces of old Nature's wondrous moods,
And all the stars of Glory's happy nights.

Lo, at the touching of his finger-tips,
   Earth's bended millions lose their burdened years,
   Unshackled slaves are masters of their fears,
And Fate destroys her serpent-woven whips;
   At his fond whispers men forget their tears
And chant the songs of God's Apocalypse!

ON THE GREAT PYRAMID.

HERE Time uplifts the curtains of the Past,
   And shows what hides behind them. Lo, I stand
   Upon the gravestones of a mighty land
Like yonder Sphinx, unspeaking to the last!
There sweep the sacred Nile's great waters vast;
   There Cairo sits; and there the Libyan sand
   Spreads shadowless. There Goshen's plains expand,
Where Jacob and his children broke their fast;
There, farther on, the ancient land of Ur,
   Whence Abram journeyed, meets the rounded sky;
Yon heaps of rubbish Memphis, Ghizeh, were,
   And here entombed old Egypt's glories lie
   Ghastly and silent, though the world comes nigh
And stirs the dust once animate in her!

IN A PUBLIC LIBRARY.

THESE walls are hero-haunted. Prisoned here
    Are princes of enchantment. King and sage,
Great knight and warrior from romantic age,
In all their wealth of glorious deeds appear.
The mad magician and the saintly seer,
    The brave and great, their mighty struggles
        wage ;
Fair ladies and base men o'er silent page
Move on forever through each changing year.

Here sleeps the fabled and here lives the true ;
    Who kept his faith and who that faith betrayed ;
        The heart of honor and the soul of shame ;
        The worthless censure reap, the worthy, fame ;
    Some bring new burdens, some their fellows aid,
But all are here, O child of joy, for you !

AT ROSSETTI'S GRAVE.

HE sleeps in sight and hearing of the sea,
    Its music and its murmurs ; fondly reach
    Incessant voices of angelic speech
Across his grave and all its mystery.
The restless waves with sounds of solemn glee
    Beat softly on the Kentish shores, and teach
    The winds that linger on the lonely beach
The songs of his exalted melody.

Great Art he served,—she was his life and light ;
　　Sweet Music sang,—she was his happiness ;
Till Glory twined his royal brows with might,
　　　And Fame's fond chorus lulled his soul's distress ;
Then Death, God's angel, came and in the night,
　　　Soothed him to slumber with Love's kind caress.

NEW ENGLAND.

NO common history hers.　Great Freedom filled
　　Her infant nostrils with the winds of power,
Love led her childish feet, and Labor thrilled
　　Her youthful yearnings into fruited flower ;
Then commonwealths and cities rose that hilled
　　　Her matron brows with Plenty's gorgeous dower,
And Art's imperial armies, service-skilled,
　　Clothed her in garbs of glory hour by hour.

Heroic children of heroic days
　　Drank virtue, faith, and valor from thy breast,
Along thy hills and valleys, brooks and bays ;
　　Then crossing prairie, scaling mountain crest,
They roamed the deserts and the lonely ways,
　　　And empires reared through all the boundless West !

IMMUTABLE.

FRET not thyself because the world and thee
  May stand in opposition. What though coarse
  Mob-hordes of error hurl invectives hoarse
And surging curse and threaten like a sea?
What though foul serpents dark with calumny
  Circle their horrid folds, and evil Force
  Chain thy poor limbs? Seek Wisdom at her Source:
If Truth be thy companion, thou art free!

One day the rabble with uncovered head
  And silent face shall gather at thy grave,
Shall heap thy tomb with Honor's holy bread
  For all the stones malignant malice gave;
Lo, there the world remorseful tears shall shed,
  And crown thee master whom it slew a slave!

THE MIGHTIEST.

MAN'S Thought is greater than his life. His soul
  Is more abiding than the nimble breath
That moves his lips with love's divine control
  And leaves them voiceless at the gates of death.
Beyond the darkened wayside where he gropes
  In mystic shadows for the paths of light,

He lives enraptured in the larger hopes
   That float before him like the stars of night.

Great Thoughts, like drum-beats in the battle, come
   To rouse through ages all the hosts of earth,
To conquer here a long millennium,
   And thrill the nations into newer birth;
Man's life is measure of a few small tears;
His Thought is endless as the ceaseless years!

LILITH.

MEN call her fair. Madonna brows of white
   With midnight hair encircled; childish eyes
   Of liquid wonders wide; uncertain-wise
Her dimpled cheeks of blossom. Jewels bright
Flood her full bosom with the stars of night;
   Soft laces billow cloud-wreaths of the skies;
   Her slightest footfalls breathe sweet melodies,
And all her movements echo music light.

But, Childhood, be thou fearful! Her desires
   Burn most voluptuous under draperies thin;
Her soul of guilty lewdness never tires;
   Her passions ravage all the hearts they win;
Her lips are crimson with the scarlet fires,
   And eat for bread the wages of her sin!

ABSENT.

I STOOD before her cottage in the gloom
   And knew it was deserted. Longings came
   And urged my drooping lips with loud acclaim
To summon her from all her ways of bloom.
Shut doors and darkened windows! O, the doom
   That weights the heart with absence of a name!
   I stood and gazed with all my senses lame
Before the temple of her silent room!

The grasses whispered, "She shall come again!"
   The roses said, "She's coming, coming soon!"
     The song-birds cried, "For us she longs and
        longs!"
For me alone no promise waited then,
   For me alone the world was out of tune,
     And silent then were all its happy songs!

PREOCCUPIED.

YES, I am strange at times, and people shake
   Their sage heads wisely at my empty face,
   My vacant eyes of wonder, and they place
Their fingers to their foreheads. Never wake
Their narrow souls with melodies that break
   In glorious music from the fields of grace;

For their rude gaze no sons of Heaven make
   Such wonders as my yearnings fondly trace.

They nothing know of where my soul is then,—
   My rapt, enraptured soul, which eye to eye
Meets visions that are seldom seen by men,—
   My soul which hears God's music pipe on high,
And feeds on raptures such as blossom when
   The child of time walks in the Bye and Bye.

A DREAM.

THIS dream is sweet,—would God it were for aye!
   My soul is clothed with freedom, and in might
   Soars upward as an angel of delight,
While there my body lies,—poor piece of clay!
Those are my friends yet living. What they say
   Sounds on my quickened senses. Helpless quite
   Am I to greet them; but these hosts in white,—
Ah, these are friends I knew but yesterday!

And am I dead? Nay, nay, but living! Those
   Who scatter tears upon the silent face
Of that still body are the dead ones! Woes
   And agonies and anguish have a place
In all the years they wander, but the rose
   Of God's eternal pleasures gives me grace!

TO ———.

I COUNT as lost the years I knew thee not,—
    The desert years that longed to know the bloom
  Of laughing springs, the summers of perfume,
And fruited autumns in each barren spot;
When all my life, with fiercest longings hot,
    And hopes unsatisfied, groped in the gloom
  Of perished fancies, and, distract with doom,
Faced horribly the future's horrid lot.

But hope smiles upward from thy laughing lips,
    Love miracles the trusting of thine eyes,
      And joy leaps at the touching of thy hands;
O, wreathe me with thy rosy finger-tips!
    For life seems heaven in the deep surprise
      Of knowing one who sees and understands!

TO ———.

THE long, dear thoughts of thee that absence brings
    Are sweet and sacred ever! How I trace
    The tender fulness of thy kindly face
Through all the dreams to which my rapture clings!
And from thy lips of happy laughter rings
    Incessant music whose mysterious grace
    Hides in my heart and finds a dwelling-place
Where all my hope with fondest fancy sings!

Fate played me false when far my feet she drew
  From thy companionship, and led me past
    The gladness and the sunshine leaping there ;
And still to-day with evils not my due
  My life from thee is held in fetters fast,
    And countless devils mock my constant prayer !

THE ONE WHO UNDERSTANDS.

SHE needs no language. Hers the soul that
    brings
  The songs of gladness for the sobbing cries,
  The smiles of rapture to the tearful eyes,
And all the grace of God's angelic things ;
Upon her lips a choir cherubic sings,
    And from her hands fall Love's divine sup-
      plies ;
  Her touch is eloquent of Paradise,
And every motion seems a throb of wings.

What sweet contentment fills the placid place
  Where calm she sits with silent lips and hands
And holds in ecstasy of rapt embrace
  The heavy heart-soul with her sweet commands !
Methinks that heaven blossoms in the face
  Of her who sees, and, seeing, understands.

SYMPATHY.

AS some great flower whose imperial bloom
    Fills all the desert with supreme delight,
And pours from heart of glory day and night
The laughing streams of purified perfume,
Yet dying droops and withers in the doom
    Hurled fiercely down from Noon's relentless
        height,—
So shrank my life in conflict, conquered quite,
Helpless and hopeless, praying for the tomb.

But one there came with kindness in her eyes,
    And on her lips the lessons angels teach ;
    She brought me dews reviving, rains that reach
From blessed fountains of benignant skies :
My veins throb wines of valor, and I rise
    Strong-armed, stout-hearted, at her tender speech!

UNFORGETTING.

AS these pale roses, crushed and faded so,
    Dry as the withered stubble, faintly keep
    The gorgeous nights of starry splendors deep,
The happy days of sunshine and their glow,—
As in their hearts the morns they used to know,
    The gentle noons and eves of shadow sleep,
    And tender odors, full of fondness, creep

From treasured fragrance of the Long Ago,—
So my poor soul, a shrivelled, worthless thing,
   Remembrance holds of half-forgotten spheres
Where first it felt the sunshine of the spring
   And drank the nectars of the golden years ;
   And now and then, between the plash of tears,
It sobs the music that it used to sing.

THE DOOR OF LIFE.

DEATH is the door of Life. There frightened flees
   The hard, ignoble world of warring creeds,
   The realm of narrow hopes and selfish deeds,
The crime and curse of murder and disease.
The small, bombastic fools that sore displease,
   The swollen knaves and microscopic breeds,
   Stay far behind, and happiness succeeds
With songs of rapture and the shades of ease.
The gods are then companions of our days,
   The noblemen of nature and the great,
      The royal hearts that found the world too small ;
And through the vast, illimitable ways,
   Where Peace and Joy, sweet servants, gladly wait,
      We walk with Truth, and Love is All in All.

INACTION.

(On account of the well-recognized precedents in such matters, the Administration does not think the present stage of affairs in Cuba justifies any change in the attitude of the Government.—*Press despatch*.)

WHAT! must thou pause, my Country, cringing low
  Before these puppets made of precedent?
  Thou unto whom the wrathful ages lent
Their swarming forces to o'ercome thy foe?
Break off thy cobweb fetters! Dost thou know
  How from thy lips imploring prayers were sent
  When thou wert feeble, till thy chains were rent
And all thine enemies met overthrow?

Arise and act! These be heroic times,
  And men are heroes when they duty do;
These precedents are idols, and all climes
  Shall worship kneeling only God the True;
  Behold thy banner waving! In its view
A sin 'gainst freedom is the worst of crimes!

TO THE RESCUE.

YEA, send thy succor quickly! Far too long,
    With heart unheeding and with palsied hands,
Great Freedom's First-born slow and slothful stands,
While armied legions 'round her neighbor throng;
Force striving after murder, fierce and strong,
    Poises the dripping dagger; thus commands
    Obeisance unto despots, and his brands
Make desolate the Ocean's Pearl with wrong!

And what though tyrants bluster? In thy youth,
    O, land of life's best longings, they cursed thee,
And thou didst fear not! Drive the wolves uncouth
    Back to their darkness, till the western sea
Rolls fetterless! Unsheathe thy sword for Truth,
    And swear, God willing, Cuba shall be free!

MISCELLANEOUS.

AT EASTERTIDE.

OVER hill and over dale,
    Over mountain, over vale,
  Hear, oh, hear
  All the music sweet and clear
From the horns of Easter blowing,
Like a river flooded flowing
  Over meadows far and near!
Wheresoe'er the echoes drift,
How the sleeping blossoms lift
In a resurrection swift
   From the horrid graves they knew
   When the winds of winter blew!
How the joyous, jocund throats
   Of the happy birds
     Open wide and fling
Outward, up, a song that floats
   Sweeter far than human words,
Full of tender, laughing notes,
    Where they soar and sing!
     'T is a time, tender time,
      Full of rich and royal rhyme,
Ever full of happy song and glee
And the mighty magic sunny of angelic melody.

Gabriel sounds his trumpet wide;
'T is the joyous Eastertide!
Yester eve the world was dead
　　In the cold embrace of night;
　　Morning brought the life and light,
And the shadows quickly fled,
And the brooding shadows far away have fled.

Over prairie, over wood,
Over all the solitude,
　　See, oh, see
　　All the buds and blossoms wee,
How they come with rapture leaping
From the heavy shadows sleeping
　　Where the storms of winter be!
When the Spring, the angel, calls
With creative voice that falls
Through the dark and dismal halls
　　Where they hidden lie asleep,
　　Suddenly they live and leap!
How their tender beauty thrills
　　With its gentle grace
　　　All the darkened earth,
All the rivers, all the rills,
With a tenderness that fills
　　Every solitary place
　　　With a newer birth!
　　　　Oh, the Spring, laughing Spring!
　　　　Ever full of joys that bring
To the wooded valley and the plain
Gorgeous glories full of spendor that shall ever-
　　　more remain!

At Eastertide.

Gabriel blows his music wide;
'T is the joyous Eastertide!
Yester eve the earth was lone
  In the winter time of wrong;
  Morning came with light and song,
And the sorrows fast have flown,
And the heavy sorrows far away have flown!

  Let the longings rule and reign
  Over heart and over brain!
    Glad and gay
    Are the songs that sound alway,
  That in chorus warble tender
  From a thousand throats of splendor
    All the bright and happy day.
Robin, lark, and linnet sing,
Wren and bluebird music bring,
Borne on swift and joyous wing
  From the sunny homes afar
  Where the balmy breezes are.
How their carols roll and rise
  As they scatter wide
    All their treasured glees,
Sweet as songs of Paradise
Underneath elysian skies,
  Till the plain and mountain-side
    Reel with melodies!
      Oh, the days, perfect days,
    When we walk in holy ways,
And the pleasant paths wherein we go
Heaven's gentle benedictions and earth's purest
    pleasures know!

Gabriel blows with pomp and pride ;
'T is the joyous Eastertide !
Yester eve the earth was sad,
   And her hills and valleys bare ;
   Morning clothed her sweet and fair,
And she trips a maiden glad,
Trips a maiden blest with beauty, who is most
      divinely clad !

Let the life be glad and gay,—
'T is the resurrection day !
   Gabriel calls
   From their ghost-enchanted halls
Every warble choice and choral,
Every blossom fond and floral,
   And the sweetest music falls !
As the flowers of beauty leap
From their cradles dark and deep,
Let thy soul in rapture sweep
   Through the aisles of glory long
   On the wings of psalm and song !
Joyous be thou in the glee
   Of the flowers that bloom,
      Of the birds that sing,
Till enchanted melody
Fills the race with revelry,
   And no shade or shadowed gloom
      Dwells within the spring !
         Time of cheer, soothing cheer !
         When millennial days are near,

Pleasures hurry onward like a flood,
And the erring ones are angels, angels that are
great and good.

Gabriel calls our souls away,—
'T is the resurrection day!
Yester eve with droop and sigh
Life was all despairing fears;
Morning wipes away our tears
In the golden Bye and Bye,
In the dreamed-of, in the sought-for, in the
longed-for Bye and Bye!

THE OLD RANGE ROAD.

ORANGE Road wide and wonderful, that
paths of heaven made
Through all the olden, golden ways where childish
fancies played,
Every inch of all your gladness is so eloquent to-day
Of all we told each other in the years that went
away!—
So eloquent of joyousness, my heart is like a prayer,
And I would fold and fondly hold and keep you
always there!

We had delightful dearnesses of rapture, you and I,
When living, in the Long Ago, the laughing Bye and
Bye,
When every mortal passing us was angel good and
wise,

That wandered out of heaven's gates and back to
    Paradise,
And all the worlds so wonderful came with them
    one and all,
And stayed with us and played with us,—but left us
    mean and small !

And how we hoped to follow them some happy day
    to come,—
Those glory-dreams of conquering, of might and
    masterdom !
We 'd march across the continent, we 'd sail across
    the sea,
And take whatever pleasured us to sceptre you and
    me ;
And all the wealth and wonder, the palace and the
    throne,
We 'd confiscate and capture and make them all our
    own !

And over you and unto me men walked miraculous,
And brought the stranger countries directly home
    to us ;
Oh, how we listened,—you and I,—to all the tales
    they told
Of Indians and of pirates, of cocoanuts and
    gold ;
And how, through all the after-dreams that haunted
    night and day,
Their anecdotes looked in again and glorified the
    way !

There was the sailor who had gone across the seas
    of calm,
And, castaway, had lived awhile amid the isles of
    palm ;
Who sported with the cannibals and taught them so
    complete
They learned at last that mission-men are never
    good to eat ;
But finally a ship hailed he, and coming to his
    home,
Found wife and children all were dead,—which
    made him love to roam !

There was the soldier who had been his country's
    stay and shield
At Winchester and Gettysburg when carnage swept
    the field ;
Who marched with Sherman to the sea and tri-
    umphed o'er the foe,
But left a leg and arm behind because of fighting
    so ;
And as he fought and marched away and told his
    tales again
The hearts of us were strangely moved to do the
    deeds of men.

And then that little fellow ! the thin, dyspeptic
    one,
Who sat and told his stories till night was nearly
    done !

He lived in big Chicago, was rich as heart's desire,
And had a wife and little ones, before the awful
　　fire;
But it burned up his family and all he had of worth,
Which sent him forth a wanderer all up and down
　　the earth.

The juggler and the showman, too, who made their
　　livings thus,
The tinman and the ragman came, and all dis-
　　coursed to us;
The Irish-linen peddler, the man who soldered tins,
Who told us all their stories of all their outs and
　　ins;
And there were scores of others whose doings large
　　and vast
Inspired to do as they did, when childhood should
　　be passed!

And so our hearts were opened, old Range Road,
　　yours and mine,
To all earth's dismal shadow and all its golden
　　shine;
And those that went along you went over me and
　　through,
And beckoned me to follow them and prove their
　　tales to you;
And so we looked with longing through happy
　　cycles when
I'd wander full of wonder down the mighty years
　　of men.

And here I am and here you are, old Comrade, much the same
As when I left you long ago to climb the hills of fame ;
I meet you and I greet you, and call you all my own
Beyond the years of vagrancy my truant feet have known ;
And in your eyes and face and hands I feel as not before
A perfectness of tenderness they never knew of yore.

The stories that they brought were true ; the wonders that they told
Revealed the world of men and things and all they have and hold ;
But after all my wanderings through all that men may do
I'm weary of their heartlessness and hasten home to you ;
And 'spite of all that's happened since, the days we used to know
Sing in my soul forevermore the songs of long ago !

There ! Let me take your hand in mine and feel your friendly face,
And lay us heart to heart again in childhood's warm embrace !

We are not old or broken down ; we both are young as when
I left the vales of childhood for the rugged hills of men ;
These hairs upon our foreheads are only white with truth,—
These tears upon our eyelids are happy tears of youth !

We used to quarrel a little. You thought me reckless quite ;
I called you old and fogy and foolish day and night :
And thus we bickered somewhat ; but after all we 've seen,
We know each other better now with fifty years between ;
For lives of work and wisdom hold never such surprise
As gazes down the future through childhood's tender eyes.

Let us forgive each other ! Of all the good and true,
I find you best and truest, and hold my heart to you ;
I hold it close and closer, and let you clasp it there
With something born of rapture between a praise and prayer ;
And through the years unending, the years of good and ill,
We 'll laugh and play together,—forever children still !

THE NIGHT.

O the Night!
When the might
Of the boundless heavens bright
Fills the hopes with satisfaction and the longings
with delight;
When the roll
And the toll
Of Life's thunders lose control,
And a wondrous diapason sounds the organs of the
soul;
And a hymn
Faintly dim
Haunts the far horizon's rim,
Like the lilt of angel music in the chants of
cherubim!

In the still
Hours that fill
Fiendish fancies full of ill,
To the innocent upwander all the wants of wish
and will;
And the wide
Fields of pride
Send their monarchs side by side

With the holy saints and martyrs that were crossed
and crucified ;
Till despair
Weights the air
With the moaning cries of care,
And the world kneels by the Father in a sin-subdu-
ing prayer !

In the weird,
Wild, and feared
Realms of silence, cherub-cheered,
How we clasp in fond embraces all that time and
toil endeared !
How the strife
Fiercely rife
With the roll of drum and fife,
Dies away in tender music of a more exalted life,
And the small
Leaps the wall
Where the less and little fall,
Till thyself is nothing, nothing, and thy God is All
in All !

Then the tears
Leave the years,
And the foolish frights and fears
List to whispers high and holy heard alone by
prophet's ears ;
And the cry,
Sob, and sigh

Leave the stricken soul for aye,
As he wanders in the wonders of the blessed Bye
and Bye;
And the woe
Demons know
In the dungeons dark below
Never shades the dreams he cherished in the happy
Long Ago!

How the gay
Raptures play,
As our ships that sailed away,
All are anchored safe at harbor in the waters of the
bay!
As the trust
Of the just
Soars above the dew and dust
Till the "may" of faith and fancy overcomes the
might of "must";
And Love drips
Pain's eclipse
From the Saviour's finger-tips,
And the world is wed to Heaven in the Lord's
Apocalypse!

O the Night!
When the might
Of the boundless heavens bright
Fills our hopes with satisfaction and our longings
with delight;

When the roll
And the toll
Of Life's thunders lose control,
And a wondrous diapason sounds the organs of the
  soul;
And a hymn
Faintly dim
Haunts the far horizon's rim,
Like the lilt of angel music in the chants of
  cherubim!

"O MY HEART, BE BRAVE AGAIN!"

O my heart,
  Be brave again!
Bear thy part
  A man of men!
These dark things of awe and error
Swift shall vanish with their terror,
  And the fears that frighten so
  Down the dying years shall go,
Till the days rejoice resplendent with the hopes that
  sweetly shine
Through the vistas of the future and its Edens
  that are thine!

What if ways
  Seem rough with wrong
Through the days
  Of sigh and song?

Thou shalt clasp the hearts that love thee,
Thou shalt climb the hills above thee,
   Thou shalt reach the land that seems
    All the heaven of thy dreams,
And a glorifying whisper shall exalt thy deepest care
To the blessed benediction of a cherub's perfect prayer.

    Drive thy fears
      And doubts away!
    Down the years
      Are pleasures gay;
These distressing clouds of sadness
Only veil the suns of gladness;
   These unholy weeds of woe
    Only hide the blooms below;
And the sun shall lift the blossoms till their tenderness shall stream
Through the laughter of thy longing and the dearness of thy dream!

    Bear the blows
      That fortune gives!
    Sorrow knows
      Each one that lives.
Be a man that bravely faces
All his failures and disgraces;
   Be a man that struggles strong,—
    Arm of might and soul of song!

Till the sceptres of the raptures thrust thy fierce detractors down,
And the world's ignoble shouters tremble at thy robe and crown!

      Joys for thee
         Shall crowding come
      In that free
         Millennium,
And the woes that weeping vex thee
Never, never shall perplex thee!
      For the years of Bye and Bye
         Shall with rapture sanctify
All the weary ways we wander through the crags of blight and blame
To the high and holy hilltops in the glory-lands of fame!

CREEDS.

TALK not to me
    Of stern decree,—
Of creeds that bind their betters;
    There is no grace
    In things that place
The human soul in fetters!

    Wake not the fear,
    Start not the tear,
That speaks of wondrous terror;

Man's heart is gold,
Its worth untold,
In spite of all his error.

No more rehearse
The priestly curse,
The ban for unbelieving;
No more condemn
The souls of them
That over guilt are grieving.

The haughty soul
Who claims control
Because of vestments holy,
Has never felt
The good that dwelt
In Christ, the meek and lowly!

In hands that feed,
In hearts that bleed,
Truth sees her greatest teacher,
Far more than all
The bans that fall
From lips of priest or preacher.

For lives that lift
The souls adrift,
The hosts of hate are yearning;
To such as know
Their grief and woe,
The sons of men are turning.

There is no creed
Like human need
To teach the grace of giving;
There is no prayer
Like tender care
To teach the love of living!

The bended knee,
It seems to me,
Is not with service gifted;
No blessings rise
From folded eyes
Unless the heart's uplifted!

Destroy the chains
That bind the brains!
'T is what we are that saves us;
No mere belief
Can conquer grief
And all the hate that braves us.

Tear up the creeds!
'T is worthy deeds,
From hands and hearts out-given,
Shall put to rout
Man's dark and doubt,
And lead him up to heaven!

THE CONQUEROR.

THE man who has found
 All the dreams that he knew,
Feels the deeds he can do!
 There is power over pain,
 There is charm for the chain,
In the hopes he has crowned
 With the garlands of gain;
 And a giant he stands
In the mystical might of his heart and his hands!

The longings that leap
 From the lips, uncontrolled,
 Are the masters of gold,
 Of the fagots and thrones,
 Of the stars and the stones,
That the multitudes keep;
 And they beckon and bring
All the glories and gifts of the pauper and king.

With hope in thy heart
 And with love in thy life,
 What is struggle or strife?
 Not a taunt nor a tear,
 Not a failure nor fear,
Not a pang nor a smart,
 Shall envenom thee here,
 Shall environ the soul
That has yielded to love and its happy control.

What matters it, then,
    Though the black of the blast
    On thy pathway be cast?
        In the truth of thy trust,
        In the might of thy "must,"
Thou shalt monarch the men
        With their dreams in the dust,
    And the stars of thy love
Shall arise in the sky as the stars rise above.

Who harvests the sheaves
    Of the grain that he sought,
    Follows ever his thought
        Through its throb and its thrill,
        Through its wonder and will,
  And the truth he believes
        Through the errors of ill;
    And he conquers at last,—
O'er the future supreme through the might of his
    past!

O Life that is long
    On the grief-laden slopes,
    Be thou true to thy hopes!
        All the dear of thy dreams,
        All the thrill of their themes,
Shall assemble in song,
        By the joy-giving streams;
    And the deeds of thy hands
Shall ennoble the races through all of the lands!

IMMORTAL.

THE life that is lived
    Never dies from the world!
On the height of the hills,
On the rush of the rills,
Over achings and ills,
    Are its banners unfurled;
And it struggles and strives
Through uncountable lives,
Till it conquering rolls
Through the darks and the deeps of unceasable souls!

The life that is lived
    Has a wonderful power!
On the mountains of might,
On the narrows of night,
On the black and the bright,
    Are its turret and tower;
Its commands have a place
In the realms of the race,
And it rules through the years
All the nations of laughter and peoples of tears.

The life that is lived
    Has unmeasured extent!

Through the present and past,
Through the vague and the vast,
From the first to the last,
    Is it centred and sent;
For its miracles reach
Over silence and speech,
Till its boundary springs
O'er the outermost edge of unendable things !

The life that is lived,—
    What a masterful thing !
How it soars in man's thought,
In the truths he has taught,
In the deeds he has wrought,
    Like a bird on the wing !
'T is an unsetting sun
Endless journeys to run,
And its blessings so hurled
That a life which is lived never dies from the world !

MIND.

NO master mine ! Eternal king
    Of Cosmos and of Chaos, I
    The awful arts of time defy,
And all diseases death may bring ;
Creation wheels her wondrous ways
    Through starry circles vague and vast,
    And age on ages hurries past,
To me as swiftly as the days.

Before dim Reason thought, I was ;
    Before the first beginnings, I
    Was monarch of the Whence and Why,
The How and Where, the primal Cause ;
Before the dreams of Time and Space,
    I ruled the empires of To Be ;
    Extent was measureless for me,
Eternity my dwelling-place !

The great, eternal, mighty Force,
    I reign, I rule, command, compel ;
    In me is Paradise and Hell,
And 'round me Nature wheels her course ;
All happiness and Truth I find,
    All Sorrows at my motion fall ;
    The Cause, the Source, the End of all,
Enduring, wondrous, deathless Mind !

An atom of myself, a thing,
    I planted in a lump of clay ;
    It grew to greatness in a day,
And called itself a man, a king ;
It caught the lightning, chained the storm,
    It felled the woods, and walked the waves,
    Explored the skies, dug earth's dim caves,
And sought to know my Face and Form.

Toward me he toils ; his golden age
    Is in the future, not the past,
    For I alone am great at last
In vacant fool or sapient sage ;

And upward, onward, shall he strive,
    This atom mine that walks the earth,
    Despising all his humble birth
And seeking me to learn, and live.

From farthest brain to farthest brain,
    While suns and stars and systems grow,
    The sovereign One above, below,
I live, I leap, I rule, I reign ;
The monarch of all things that are,
    Of all that is and is to be,
    My sceptre leaps with forces free
From sun to sun and star to star !

DREAMER AND SINGER.

THE world laughed long at his pensive face
    And the wistful gaze of his tender eyes,
But he knew the glint of a wondrous grace
    And the perfect pleasures of Paradise ;
And the scenes he saw were so fair and bright
    That the wise men longed for the fond array ;
For an angel dreamed in his heart by night,
    And a little bird sang in his soul by day.

The words of his mouth made a music sweet
    That rippled and rang with the notes of glee,
And sad hosts echoed the strains replete
    With all of their rhythmical rhapsody ;

And he sang a song, till they knew his might,
    Till they kissed his feet on the public way ;
For an angel dreamed in his heart by night,
    And a little bird sang in his soul by day.

His years were happy with joys divine,
    And his longings lived in a far-off land ;
And sweeter than drops of the sweetest wine
    Were the hopes he only could understand ;
And all the hours of his days were light,
    And all the loves of his life were gay ;
For an angel dreamed in his heart by night,
    And a little bird sang in his soul by day.

There are gifts divine that are more than great,
    And prouder than sceptres that monarchs wear ;
And what to him were the pomp of state
    And the tinselled splendor that glittered there ?
The sorrows and troubles from him took flight,
    And the tears at his coming fled far away ;
For an angel dreamed in his heart by night,
    And a little bird sang in his soul by day.

What mattered it, then, if a ragged coat
    And a broken cap were the garbs he wore ?
That crusts were his food ? For he sang the note
    Of a tender song, and he wept no more !
And we know, we know, that his love was bright,
    That his life was the roll of a roundelay ;
For an angel dreamed in his heart by night,
    And a little bird sang in his soul by day.

And he is greater than czars and kings!
  The world may praise them awhile in fear,
But wreathes its laurels for him who sings
  And soothes the anguish of toil and tear;
And he is enthroned on Love's far height
  While kingdoms crumble and crowns decay;
For an angel dreams in his heart by night,
  And a little bird sings in his soul by day!

THE ROSES.

WHAT do the roses know
    Of the noon and the night?
What of the dark through which they grow
    Up to the life and light?
Above are the stars and the dew,
    Below are the soil and the sod;
How it happened they never knew,
    But they sprang from stone and clod!

What do the roses know
    Of the shriek and the song?
What of the breeze that blesses so,
    What of the gale that is strong?
Above are the skies of the bright,
    Below are the seas of the shade,
And full of beauty by day and night
    Do their hot cheeks flush and fade.

What do the roses know
    Of the dreams that they dream?
What of the fancies that spring and flow
    Forth in a bountiful stream?
They bud and they blossom and die,
    They wither and shrivel and fade;
Does all they were in the ashes lie
    Where the petals low are laid?

What do the roses know
    Of the dead or the dust?
What of a life where they shall blow
    Glad as the garlands of trust?
Do they at the touch of the hand
    With rapture astart and athrill,
Feel joys their hearts cannot understand
    That are strong as wish and will?

What do the roses know?
    We are all of the truth!
Life that is red in their hearts aglow,—
    Is life of my life, in sooth!
The dreams they dream in the dew
    Are dreams that I cannot control,—
These hopes of mine are the hopes that grew
    In the depths of a rose's soul!

What do the roses know?
    They are peers of the wise;
Ever they struggle from earth below,
    Ever they long for the skies!

They prize the dreams of a darling hope,
    As much as the children of men,
And here and there on a sunny slope
    I shall meet them all again !

GREED.

WHEREVER the man upturns the soil,
    Wherever he sows the seed,
There dwells a monster that mocks his toil,
    And the monster's name is Greed !
And year by year, as men garner in
    The harvest they reap in pain,
The monster sits by the bursting bin,
    And he feasts on the golden grain.

There is never a home in the world so wide
    That is far from his haunts away ;
If he shuns the palace with all its pride,
    Yet he enters the hut to stay ;
And where the race in its sorrow strives
    On the barren heath or hill,
He claims his armies of human lives
    And his legions of human will.

He gathers the rose from the rounded cheek
    And the red from the rare young lip,
And the strongest arm in the world is weak
    At the touch of his finger-tip ;

And the happy song is a mournful wail,
  And the laugh is a shriek of fright;
For the world grows fierce and is thin and pale
  In the awe of his appetite.

Then Sin with her bitter herbs of grief,
  And Vice with her potions wild,
With ready promise of long relief
  Win woman and man and child!
For what is Virtue when want is near,
  And what is the fairest fame?
They are all undone at the doom they hear
  In the shriek of the monster's name!

It's Oh, for the tears that are nightly shed
  When he cometh to claim his own!
And Oh, for the curses that heap his head
  Where the millions of men make moan!
It's Oh, for the children that helpless cry,
  For the women that wail and weep,
A-faint for the crust that his hands deny
  And the crumb that his fingers keep!

Then ho, for the hero with shining shield
  And a spear like the lance of God,
To whose hard blow shall the monster yield,
  And the curse of the toiler's sod!
A thousand ages of glory stay
  For the Knight of the Noble Deed,
For the strong, brave heart who shall come and slay
  The monster of human Greed!

PLAYING HORSE.

UP and down the pathway lined
    With sweet grasses intertwined,
Where the orchard's bud and bloom
Fill the air with fond perfume,
Rides a hero brave and bold
As the fabled knights of old,
On a charger that he deems
Wondrous as his wondrous dreams!

Firm he sits the reins to clasp
More securely in his grasp;
Swift the spurs descending clank
Deeply in the tender flank;
Cruel swings the savage whip,
Pliant to his finger-tip,
And his charger gallops gay
'Round the wonder world away!

Forth he journeys fast and far
Where the gnomes and fairies are,
And he gladly enters in
Lands where happy dreams begin!
Lingers he a little while
Where the pleasures bow and smile;

Then away around the ring!
'T is the land where Fun is king!

Oh, the happy birds that throng
All the ways he hastes along,
And the gorgeous flowers that blow
Over every land below!
And each little boy, with curls
Dear and dainty as a girl's,
Stands with playthings waiting for
Every little visitor!

Tired, he ceases from his quest!
Horse and rider both may rest!
Now the steed that galloped gay
Munches at the brambled hay;
But the rider, never still,
Restless in his wish and will,
Dreams a greater dream and then
Calls himself a man of men!

Ah, my little dreamer, we
All are dreams in some degree,
And we learn as on we go
Dreams are dearest things we know!
Blest if over blooming meads
We may ride our gallant steeds,
Till, life ended, o'er the hill
Forth we venture dreaming still!

A GLAD PLAYFELLOW.

THERE'S a happy little fellow
   I am sure you'd like to meet,
For his ways are all so pleasant
   And his manners are so sweet;
And his greetings are so hearty,
   And his words so joyous, too,
That I know you'd run to meet him
   If he'd show his face to you.

There was never yet a person
   Ever looked into his face,
Ever touched his rosy fingers,
   Ever saw his joyous grace,—
That would want to be without him,
   That would leave him far or say
He is not the best playfellow
   That has ever come his way.

Oh, his hair is glad and golden,
   And his eyes are brightly blue,
And his features are as handsome
   As the fairies ever knew;
And his lips are happy ever
   In the music that he sings,

For he finds the perfect pleasures
In the most imperfect things.

He is most accommodating,
    For whate'er your age and size
He can make the things about you
    Always pleasant, if he tries;
And whatever wish you cherish
    He will make your fortune fit,
Till you clap your hands delighted
    At the gladsomeness of it!

It is true that you may miss him
    As you wander down the years,
But you 're pretty sure to find him
    In among the toils and tears;
For in unexpected places
    Where you never thought to see,
He is oftenest appearing
    With his happy face of glee.

But I know if you should meet him
    You will find him quite so fair
That your heart can ne'er forget him,
    But will follow everywhere;
It will follow him forever
    Through the worlds below, above,
For his dwelling-place is Pleasure;
    And his name?—his name is Love!

THE ON-MARCH.

LO, Progress is no swift release from error,
   No sudden sun that banishes the night;
Through weary cycles, Man, the burden-bearer,
   Gropes in the dark and struggles toward the light.

'T is not in death-throes where the battle rages,
   And nations heap the winrows of their slain,
That Freedom leaps across the darkened ages,
   And Truth unchains the bondmen of the plain.

And from the fields where armies meet despoiling,
   No love-born carols hush the cries of wrong;
But, through the yearning years with anguish toiling,
   Man makes himself the instrument of song.

Lo, where the tireless thinker works and wonders,
   Where Man and God in fellowship unite,
There leaps the Thought to majesty that thunders
   Through endless ages with unceasing might!

Some seer, enraptured at his dreams of duty,
   In grave speech frames a precept or a law,
And years long after mankind lives in beauty
   The gorgeous glories that the prophet saw!

Some teacher from his closet tells the nations
   The words of Truth, the Deeds that men should
      do ;
And they through sorrows and deep tribulations
   Toil fiercely on to prove his lessons true !

Man's Mind is greater than his brawn or bullet ;
   His Thought far vaster than his Labor stands ;
Men's hopes are higher than the world, and rule it,—
   Their hearts are stronger than their helpless
      hands !

Development unwearied outward courses
   Through deepest darkness with unresting tides ;
Brain-throbs and heart-beats are the deathless
      forces
   That lead us, lift us, where the day abides.

Still up and onward, up and forward, surges
   The toiling race, near-drawing to the goal,
While Truth with whips of righteous anger urges
   The craven fool to prove a Master Soul.

Quote not the past ! Its regal courts were rabble,
   A puny herd of worse than worthless things ;
The world moves upward from their childish bab-
      ble,—
   The tireless toilers are the only kings !

Yea, Man himself, the fruit of long endeavor,
   Grows from the smallness of his ancient youth,
And shall, at last perfected, stand forever
   An angel shaped and fashioned to the Truth !

THE DREAMER.

HE dreamed a dream ; and far his hopes
    Went roaming o'er the mountain slopes ;
They climbed the summits coldly tall,
They crossed the high horizon's wall,
And lingered where the morning star
Illumined royal realms afar ;—
Men shook their heads : " He is unfit
For life," they said. What mattered it ?
    He dreamed a dream.

He dreamed a dream ; and in his soul
He heard mysterious music roll ;
He saw sweet visions weirdly rise
Before the longings of his eyes,
And knew the good of Man eclipse
The joys of God's Apocalypse ;—
They said : " He has nor wish nor will " ;
He heeded not ; what matter still ?
    He dreamed a dream !

He walked the ways in rags that felt
The horrid homes in which he dwelt ;
And now and then in lonely days
He sang some simple roundelays,

Until the hungry, hardened throngs
Knew something of his tender songs;—
"On foolish things his heart is set,"
The thousands said. No matter yet!
    He dreamed a dream!

And lo, he lost his dream, and died,
To find it on the other side!
And o'er his coffin bent a few
With hearts of grief and eyes of dew,
Till they a vision saw, and sought
The music that he tamed and taught;
And year by year a grateful throng
Bows low to bless the Man of Song
    Who dreamed a dream.

Ah, life is more than tears or toil,
Its wages more than sin or soil,
And from its holy hands are shed
Diviner gifts than blows or bread;
Who dreams a dream is greater far
Than crowds and crowns and kingdoms are,
And stars and skies and systems roll
To palm and praise the mystic soul
    That dreams a dream!

THE STARS.

STARS and the seas of the night!
  Stars and the deeps of the dawn!
And the dim of the dusk is athrob with the light
  For the ships that are sailing on!
What if the hurricanes blow?
  What of the billow and blast?
The harbor waits, and the sailors know
  They shall anchor in port at last.

Life and the power of its pain;
  Life and the doom of its death;
And the ghastly ghosts of the wandering slain
  With their foul and pestilent breath!
What if it sicken and fall?
  What if it wither and die?
It only goes to the All in All
  In the worlds of the Bye and Bye.

Love and the joys of its trust;
  Love and the gold of its gain;
And the agonies fierce when its blossoms are dust
  And its raptures have perished in pain!
What if it wander and weep?
  What if it murmur and moan?
The heart of the Master is never asleep,
  And the lover shall come to his own.

Man and the might of his hope ;
   Man and the curse of his care ;
And the footsteps that falter and fingers that grope
   In the dim and the dusk of despair !
What if he stumble and fail ?
   What if he perish, in sooth ?
The lights are above him ; at last he shall scale
   All the hills of the true and the Truth !

Stars and the seas of the night !
   Stars and the deeps of the dawn !
And the dim of the dusk is athrob with the light
   For the ships that are sailing on !
What if the hurricanes blow ?
   What of the billow and blast ?
The harbor waits, and the sailors know
   They shall anchor in port at last !

THE LITTLE BOY'S HAIR.

HIS mother and I cut the little boy's hair !
   Hair that grew where the years begin,
Bright and sunny and fondly fair
   As the baby dreams it was tangled in !
And tears came into our eyes that day,—
   Tears for the baby that left us then,—
For oh, we knew when he went away
   He never would come to our home again !

His mother and I cut the little boy's hair!
    Twisted curls that the fairies made,
Hung by his brows in the breezes where
    The blessed feet of the children played!
It woven was with the fancies true,
    The hopes that ever with childhood dwell,
And held the joys that our baby knew,
    The low, sweet laughter he loved so well!

His mother and I cut the little boy's hair!
    Faces grave with a grief sublime,
Eyes so guilty they would not dare
    To look aloft as we did the crime!
Our hands upgathered the golden glow,
    They clutched the glories miraculous!
What vandals we! But he could not know
    The deep emotions that mastered us!

His mother and I cut the little boy's hair!
    "You," we whispered, "are now a man!"
Mourning deep in our hearts the rare
    Sweet grace that grew where the years began!
And all that day there were tears that shone
    Within the lids of our tender eyes,
And soft we wept to ourselves alone
    Where none could enter and sympathize.

His mother and I cut the little boy's hair!
    Life is longer than children know;
Day by day there is more of care
    Than heaped the hearts of the Long Ago!

For these are the curls that we cut off then,
   As dear as the boy with his dreams of Good,
Who laid them by for the toils of men,
   In the long-lost years of his babyhood!

THE LITTLE DEAD BABY.

THERE'S a little dead baby just over the way,
   For a little white ribbon hangs down by the door,
And the house that was happy with music and play
   Is encompassed with gloom and rejoices no more;
And the shutters are closed and the curtains are drawn,
   And the bird by the window is songless to-day;
For the bright of the blossoms went out at the dawn
   With the little dead baby just over the way.

There's a little dead baby just over the way,
   And a little white coffin all hidden from view;
And a poor little mother kneels lowly to pray
   By the beautiful face of the baby she knew;
But the Lord of her soul with a gladness unguessed
   To her heart gives a joy that shall anguish allay;
And her faith lives as pure as the blooms on the breast
   Of the little dead baby just over the way.

There's a little dead baby just over the way,
   And a desolate look never noticed before;

And the children are silent, and tearfully say,
  "The baby won't laugh at our pranks any more!"
And the old people walk with a sorrowful tread
  As the tears of regret down the faded cheeks stray,
For they worshipped each hair on the bright curly head
  Of the little dead baby just over the way.

There's a little dead baby just over the way,
  And the hushes of awestricken silences throng
Through the jest of the crowd and the merriment gay
  With the rapture and revel of laughter and song;
And the world bows its head with a sorrowful face
  Where the stars of compassion their glories array,
While the angels come down full of love to the place
  Of the little dead baby just over the way.

Oh, the little dead baby just over the way!
  There's a Presence that clothes it with dearness divine;
And I feel in my heart the omnipotent sway
  Of the grief I should know if that baby were mine!
And I mourn with the mourning, and ask from above
  That the Father will comfort when sorrows dismay,
While my soul is a fountain that flows full of love
  For the little dead baby just over the way!

RENUNCIATION.

KISS me, love, before you leave me !
    Here the cherished hope shall end ;
I shall bravely, though it grieve me,
    Lose the lover in the friend !
Forward where your longings lift you !
    Nay, I 'll never bar the way !
May the joyous breezes drift you
    To the harbor lights of day !

Kiss me, love, before you leave me !
    To your heart once fold me fast !
Though the future may deceive me,
    I shall treasure still the past !
What shall matter wintry weather ?
    Memory is deathless youth ;
We shall tread the years together,
    Down the dewy slopes of truth !

Kiss me, love, before you leave me !
    These poor tears of mine are naught,
Yet this parting shall bereave me
    Of the dearest things I thought ;
But nor will nor wish may falter !
    Shall the wooed be less than wife ?
Here I lay upon the altar
    All the longings of my life !

Kiss me, love, before you leave me !
  These are only foolish themes !
May the price I pay achieve me
  Crowns for all your hopes and dreams ;
But remember what was given :
  One sad woman slew her love,
Faced her fate, and left her heaven,—
  You shall gain the heights above !

Kiss me, love, before you leave me !
  Here the cherished hope shall end ;
I shall bravely, though it grieve me,
  Lose the lover in the friend !
Forward where your longings lift you !
  Nay, I 'll never bar the way !
May the joyous breezes drift you
  To the harbor lights of day !

"THERE, MY HEART, BE STILL A MINUTE."

THERE, my heart, be still a minute ;
  Don't you worry so !
There 's a song if we begin it
  Everywhere we go !
What if days of happy boy-time
  Never come again ?
We shall find the perfect joy-time
  Down the ways of men !

"There, my Heart, Be Still a Minute."

When the darkest hours are over,
    Morn with fingers bright
Shall the sweetest blooms discover,
    Grown within the night;
Never ruin, but entwined it
    Vines of sympathy;
Never cloud, but stars behind it
    Lit the tender sky!

Yours and mine is friendship stronger
    Than the world receives;
You and I are comrades longer
    Than the world believes;
You rejoice in all my gladness,
    Every laugh I know;
Let me banish all your sadness,—
    Don't you worry so!

Let your lips forget to quiver;
    Brush the tears away!
Never hour but was a giver
    Of the glad and gay!
What's the use of getting gloomy,
    When the skies are blue?
All the meadow lands are bloomy
    For the likes of you!

There, my heart, be still a minute;
    Don't you worry so!
There's a song if we begin it
    Everywhere we go!

What if days of happy boy-time
  Never come again?
We shall find the perfect joy-time
  Down the ways of men!

A RAMBLE.

WE wandered with fond feet beyond the town
    And all the stifled streets of dust and
      smoke,
Until we rested in the country fields.

It was a place where angels might have walked :
A rounded vale of solitude and song,
That weary souls of longing fondly dream
When fainting with the fevers of their toil
And bending with the burdens of the years.
Green slopes of summer grasses, kindly wreathed
With speckled lawns of clovers red and white,
Spread their soft carpets on the bounding earth
Where playful sheep and lowing cattle grazed.
An infant stream with limpid waters low
Crept slowly through the mossy margins wide,
And singing kissed the pebbles with kind lips
That lingered on the ripples. Far above,
The ancient, gabled mill with throbbing wheels
Beat sombre music from the careless waves.
A brooding elm hung over, in whose shade
The sultry hours of sleepy silence wane,
And all the heart's dear yearnings are at rest.

Birds in the scattered trees companionless
Heaped lullabies upon the tender air,
While wide-winged swallows touched the water's
    breast
And twittered in their merry ecstasies.
Some lonely quail with cheerful whistle called
His absent comrade from the bearded field.
While over all the arching sky of blue
In rapture caught the valley in its arms
And smoothed the tiny wrinkles from its brow.

And there we two, the friends of other years
When life was in the distance of our dreams,
Lay on the grasses all that summer day
And talked again of joys we used to know,
Of longings crushed and tender hopes that died,
And years that fled as dreams go down the night;
Till shadows brought the dewy breath of eve
And twilight drove us from the lovely scene,
With such fond pleasures ringing in our hearts
As cheered our bosoms in the times of yore,
When boyhood looked beyond his foolish ways
And dreamed of glory in the years to be.

UNFORGETTING.

FORGET thee, dearest? Till the tide
    Forgets the orb that lifts the sea,
My heart shall leap with naught beside
    Abiding thoughts of thee,—of thee!

Until the rose forgets the dew
    That cools and feeds with fine control,
My soul shall know, as once it knew,
    The raptures of a kindred soul.

Till longing sleeps and love is dead
    And darkness falls and griefs destroy,
My heart shall treasure all we said
    And hold our happy hopes of joy.

Through all the days I wander where
    Thy presence makes a Paradise;
Through all the nights I slumber there
    Beneath the heavens of thine eyes.

Though suns should leap across our ways
    And starry systems intervene,
My soul would break each bond that stays,
    And scale the heights that rise between.

What if a thousand worlds upheave?
    The lover's heart will find his own,
And, though a storm-tossed absence grieve,
    He clasps her, and is not alone.

Each moment I caress thy face,
    Each moment feel thy hands in mine,
Each moment in thy close embrace
    I thrill with kisses thrice divine.

And all the hours from dark to dawn,
   And all from dawn to dark, I see
Thy darling face, and wander on
   Enchanted paths that lead to thee.

Nay, dear, think not I can forget;
   The days may hasten o'er the hill,
The nights may come with darkness, yet
   My heart shall hold thee,—hold thee still!

THE MINOR CHORD.

    A sweet bird sings
In prison shadows where the griefs are sorest,
    And gladly rings
The wondrous music of his native forest;
    But all his songs
Breathe evermore some minor strain of sadness,
    And through them throngs
No more the old free melody of gladness;
      For something sobs and sighs
      In every song he tries.
His lay seems quite the sweetest ever heard,
    But oh, the bird, the bird!

    A singer sings,
Far from the days of childhood glad and golden,
    Fantastic things
The angels taught him in the cycles olden;
    But anguish dwells

In every strain his throbbing bosom utters,
  And sorrow swells
In every note that from him falls and flutters ;
  In every song he knows
  Sob life's unceasing woes.
They say his harmonies forever linger ;
  But oh, the sad, sad singer !

  There are no songs
Praiseworthy save the singer's heart has known
    them ;
  Their truth belongs
Alone and only to the lives that own them !
  In every note
Of touching tenderness that overmasters,
  Divinely float
The voiceless anthems of unnamed disasters,—
  In every perfect strain,
  Some hope that died in pain !
Do they forget, who crown the ones that bring them,
  The prices paid to sing them ?

IN THE NIGHT.

OH, the stillness and the sweetness of the night !
  How the soul arousing rises from the mysteries of dreams,
Ere the beautifying brightness of the morning's purple light
  Through the golden vales of glory like a flooded river streams !

Then the hand of some glad angel with a tender
        touch unbars
    All the fairy fields of fancy with unfading blooms
        bedight,
And we wander there as happy as the twinkles of
        the stars,
    In the stillness and the sweetness of the night.

In the stillness and the sweetness of the night
    Comes a holier inspiration than the days can ever
        know,
And seraphic shapes of shadow in their glory-
        garments white
    Summon memories of music from the lyric Long
        Ago ;
Oh, the gates of heaven open, and the happy hosts
        of joy
    Soothe the heart away from sorrow with their
        melodies of might,
Till the years are young forever and the old man is
        a boy,
    In the stillness and the sweetness of the night !

In the stillness and the sweetness of the night
    Faintly sound the witching murmurs of a thou-
        sand eerie things
From the thrilling throats of darkness on the forest-
        haloed height
    And the leaping lips of laughter where the rest-
        less river sings ;

Oh, the voices of the ages God's prophetic lessons teach
  To the heavy heart that hungers for the rhapsodies of right,
And the secrets of the silence lisp their hopes in happy speech,
  In the stillness and the sweetness of the night !

In the stillness and the sweetness of the night,
  Oh, the soul breaks out of prison in a glorified release
From the fetters of its weakness and the bondage of its blight,
  To the blessed benedictions and the plenitudes of peace !
And on wings of joyous rapture, far among the great and good,
  How it soars with love and longing to its ancient palace bright,
And beholds cherubic wonders only known and understood
  In the stillness and the sweetness of the night !

SAVE THE BOYS.

SAVE the boys; they make the treasures!
   Vain is all thy strain and striving,
Worthless all thy narrow measures
   Made to further thrift and thriving.
Souls are priceless; of thy brother,
   Of his sons, thou art the keeper;
Save the boys; endeavors other
   Are unworthier and cheaper.

Save the boys; they make the nations!
   Haste the marches up and onward;
Banish all the fierce temptations
   From the paths we travel dawnward;
Laws can break each galling fetter;
   Love can lift from shame and scorning,
Save the boys; and purer, better
   Men shall reach the Gates of Morning.

Save the boys; they make the future!
   Hearts and lives and hopes are pleading
For the death of sins that nurture
   Curse and crime for hosts succeeding;
Millions low in prayer are craving
   Good which fills the earth with leaven;
Save the boys; and in their saving,
   Save the human race for heaven!

Save the boys; they make the ages!
   Conquer Vice with Virtue's rigor;

Battle brutishness like sages ;
  Swing the scythe of Truth with vigor.
Duty, now ! Be coward never !
  Time shall tell thy fame in story ;
Save the boys ; the Great Forever
  Looks to thee and them for glory !

TAKE IT EASY !

TAKE it easy ! What 's the use
  Of your haste and hurry ?
Life can offer no excuse
  For the waste of worry ;
When you get to mixing things
  Hope becomes a bubble,
For there 's never heart that sings
  O'er the tears of trouble.

Take it easy ! He that frets
  Never knows the pleasures,
And the richest poorest gets
  In love's golden treasures ;
If to sadness you are cold,
  She from you will sever ;
Treat her kindly, and the old
  Jade will stay forever !

Take it easy ! Life 's a crown,—
  Like a monarch wear it ;
If a burden weight it down,
  Happy be and bear it !

Drink the nectars from the skies,
  Which the gods bequeath you!
And in rapture you shall rise
  Leaving earth beneath you!

Flowers of beauty bloom and bless
  All the ways you wander,
And the songs of blessedness
  Chime from over yonder.
Don't get blue! The world is bright,
  Beautiful, and breezy;
Life is but one long delight
  If,—you take it easy!

MY LOVE.

I CRIED with a cry to my love;
  And my soul with a jubilant thrill
Strode over the oceans between her and me,
  And over the mountains of ill;
But never an answer arose from her lips,
  And never a joyous reply
Came out of the distance and tenderly hushed
  The terrible sob of the cry.

I prayed with a prayer to my love;
  And high on the wings of its hope
My heart hurried far through the valleys of time
  And over eternity's slope;
But she uttered no word where the silences lay
  To banish my yearning despair,

And lost in the seas where the surges are vast
  Were the throbs of my desperate prayer.

I sang with a song to my love,
  Under the stars and the night,
And the feet of my song o'er the ways of the world
  Sped swift in their longings for light ;
And when she drew near in the purples of dawn,
  It seemed I had known her so long,—
This heart of my heart and this soul of my soul
  That heeded my summons of song !

Not the terror of cry, not the pathos of prayer,
  Did she hear in the silences wide,
But she hastened away at the carols of song
  With her jubilant feet to my side ;
I know not, I know not, the land or the sea,
  The mountain or stream she had known ;
I know not the path that she came,—but I know
  That she came, and is only my own !

A HEALTH.

YOUR health as you leave us !
  We know what you think,—
Yes, that is man's Babel,—
  No wonder you shrink !
'T is right to be happy ?
  Aye, truly, I hold,
And life has more in it
  Than laurels and gold.

Then up with life's cup,—
    Here's a bumper to gladden!
May the sorrows that dance
On the highways of chance
    Never gather so near as to sadden;
Wherever you linger, wherever you stray,
May roses and lilies entangle your way!

It is joy that I wish you,
    Unclouded by care;
It is crowning of purpose,
    Fulfilling of prayer;
It is all that you hope for
    And all that you deem
The love of your longing,
    The dear of your dream!

Then up with life's cup!
    There is wine in the chalice!
Let us rouse us a laugh
As we cheerily quaff
    Like a thirsty old king in his palace.
Your health, your good health! 'T is enough
    for your worry
To capture the pleasures as onward you hurry.

LONELINESS.

DEAD she is, and the glowing embers
    Fancy fired in the olden days
All are ashes, and life remembers
    Few, indeed, of her words and ways.

It was eve and the year was vernal,
   Soft the breeze, and the sky was fair,—
Hearts are hungry and love eternal,—
   Oh, the tints of her face and hair!

Slow we walked with our happy faces
   Down the deeps of the darkened gloom,
And our souls in their love-embraces
   Wedded there in the orchard bloom.

It was nothing! A hand-clasp only,
   Just a kiss in the shadows low;
But my heart when she went was lonely,
   And I wept in my sorrow so.

It was nothing! But from me never
   Lifts the touch of her tender lips;
Through my veins there will romp forever
   Thrills that fell from her finger-tips!

It was nothing! We parted,—parted,—
   Ne'er to meet in the world again;
She with love of the good glad-hearted,
   I so sad with the griefs of men.

Dead she is, and she lies out yonder
   Cold as the gravestones are and white;
But forever our souls shall wander
   Hand in hand through the fields of light!

IN MEMORY OF EUGENE FIELD.

(Died Nov. 4, 1895.)

WELL, bear the empty cage away ;
    Our lips with wondrous woes are white ;
The bird that warbled all the day
    Has left us lonely in the night.

He sang of fields and orchard blooms,
    And groves that gave delightful shade ;
Of perfect flowers whose fond perfumes
    Fell where delighted children played.

The raptures of the homely joys
    Romped in his tender roundelays,
And fun and frolic like a boy's
    Beside him wandered all his ways.

Glad children paused from play to hear
    The pipes melodious that he blew,
And Age with happy step drew near
    To know forgotten dreams anew.

His music waked the smiles that leap
    From joyous deeps of angel eyes,
And held the hopes that happy creep
    From hearts as pure as Paradise.

The race has lost a fondest friend,
　　The children one that laughed with them,
The countless hosts in sorrow blend
　　Their sobs to sound his requiem.

Yes, bear the empty cage away!
　　Our lips with wondrous woes are white;
The bird that warbled all the day
　　Has left us lonely in the night.

A SUPPLIANT.

O GOD! When Dreams of Good are dead,
　　And buried low they lie,—
When Hope is gone and Love is fled,—
　　Then let me die!

The heart may sing o'er faded flowers,
　　Beside the bursting leaf;
But tears unceasing sob the hours
　　Of Winter's grief.

The soul with lofty courage weds
　　Where mountains meet the sun,
But where the prairie's level spreads
　　It sinks undone.

The night with all its wail and woe,
　　Bleak winds and bitter skies,
Forgets the darkness if it know
　　The morn shall rise.

Life undismayed can feel the thorn
    And walk the plains by night,
If blossom, mountain-side, and morn
    Be still in sight.

When dreams of better things are dead,
    And buried low they lie,—
When Hope is gone and Love is fled,—
    Then let me die!

MOTHERHOOD.

MOTHERHOOD! Motherhood!
    More than any brotherhood,
More than any other hood
    Underneath the skies;
Let me sing a song to you,
Glad and true and strong to you,
Till the stars belong to you,
    Earth and Paradise!

More than glees and gratitudes
Are your sweet beatitudes,
Born in Heaven's latitudes,
    Where the joys abide;
Angel hearts that treasure you
Ever come to pleasure you,
Bringing gifts that measure you
    With the glorified.

Then a happy song to you
While the joys belong to you

And no shade of wrong to you
　　Floods the days with tears !
Motherhood ! Motherhood !
More than any brotherhood,
More than any other hood,
　　Laughing through the years !

THE COMMONPLACES.

AH, the childish commonplaces ! Like the old
　　　familiar faces,
　How they peep forever outward from the skies of
　　　Long Ago,
And their rhapsodies of laughter follow fondly on
　　　and after
　All the winding ways of glory that our fairest
　　　fancies know !

Oh, the happy commonplaces ! How remembrance
　　　interlaces
　In the sombre soul of shadow all the shine it
　　　ever knew,
Till the yearning years of sorrow from their blessed
　　　brothers borrow
　All the raptures that with magic throw a halo
　　　over you !

And the joyous commonplaces ! How their music
　　　madly races
　Through the heart and soul aweary, and the joys
　　　abiding brings ;

For from out the gates of golden, from the cycles
    bright and olden,
  Comes the angel of Jehovah with the cherubim
    and sings!

And the careless commonplaces! Full of laugh-
    ter's gladdest graces,
  How the murmurs of their voices fall across the
    ways we go,
And the carols they are singing, rich and royal
    chorus bringing,
  Soothe the bruises of the battle and the weary
    wounds of woe!

Oh, from you I cannot sever! And forever and
    forever
  I shall drink your magic music, gaze upon your
    forms divine,
Till again with glad embraces we shall meet, O
    Commonplaces,
  And shall wander on unwearied where the stars
    of heaven shine!

JOY ABIDES.

THE Troubles are feathers that flee
  O'er Pleasure's unchangeable sea,
The bubbles that darken the wave,
  The brambles that tangle the wild;
But Hope is a blossom that gladdens the grave,
  And Life is the laugh of a child.

The Sorrows that sadden us here
Like mists of the morn disappear ;
For Joy with her light and her love
    Fills all of the world with her glees,
And mortals in ships that are launched from above
    Sail over eternity's seas.

Then sing all the lullabies long
That Pleasure is crooning in song !
They silence the clatter and din
    That echo where error has trod ;
If Hate be as old as the demons of sin,
    Yet Love is enduring as God !

THE HOURS.

WITH bandaged eyes beside the way I stood,
    Where one by one in swift procession passed
The muffled hours and tossed their gifts at me,—
Crowns, kingdoms, stars, and what they all contain.
They mocked my hands that beat the darkness there,
Reclaimed their bounties, and with savage scorn
And taunts of bitterness went o'er the hills.
But all was not denied me ; as I clutched
In deep anxiety of groping hands,
I caught some ribbon, rose, or wisp of hair,
Some screed of song, some sentence of the heart,

Some child's fond plaything sanctified with love,
But mourned for crowns my blindness could not
    gain.
And when my heart was weary with its years,
Then Wisdom came and made mine eyes to see ;
And lo, my trinkets were the keys of life,
More precious than the stars for which I wept !

UNDISMAYED.

AS long as the Spring with her blossoms
    Bends over the beautiful lea,—
As long as the bird with its music
    Sings all of its carols for me,—
My soul for its longings shall struggle,
    My Hope battle on with a will,
Till the blossoms of Spring are all faded,—
    The bird and its music are still !

As long as the song of the singer
    Sounds over the valleys of earth,—
As long as the lips of the lover
    Are red with the raptures of mirth,—
My heart shall renew its endeavor,
    My life in its longing shall trust,
Till the song of the singer is weary,
    And Love is a dream of the dust !

ALAS, MY OWN HARP!

ALAS, my own Harp! In the shadows of night
  'T is our fortune to sing all the numbers we
    know,
And murmur in darkness the songs of delight
  That shall soften our sadness and weaken our
    woe.
But cease not thy strains! We forever will pour
  From the deeps of our days, full of yearning and
    youth,
Though Fame should encircle our brows never-
    more,
  Sweet songs that are happy with honor and truth!

Let the strains of thy measures unceasingly flow,
  Though marred in their music by murmurs of
    mine;
Should Glory ne'er crown them, 't will cheer thee to
    know
  Love hath blest with her roses these carols of
    thine;
Then sway the sweet strings! Let the melodies
    move
  With the raptures that never seem harsh or un-
    couth;
Some heart full of longing shall listen and prove
  How great are the songs of thine honor and truth!

FAITH.

LIKE a comet strange and wild,
    Through the trackless regions vast
Reels the Soul from ages past,
God's companion, Heaven's child;
Nothing tells it of the great
    Planets where it rolled and whirled;
Nothing knows it of the fate
    That has flung it on the world.
Here it wanders dark or dim
    Till it creeps apart alone,
Past the far horizon's rim
    Through eternities unknown;
But He brought it from the deep,—
He will all its wanderings keep,
And it never once shall move
From His law or from His love!

BENEATH THE PINES.

BENEATH the Pines on drowsy wings,
    My sleepy hammock sways and swings,
While through half-open, half-shut eyes
    Creep lazily the far-off skies
And all the world that sobs and sings.

From Music's feather-throated kings,
A perfect chorus rising rings

And soothes me with its lullabies,
  Beneath the Pines.

O happy hours! An angel brings
Glad visions of divinest things,
  Where half asleep I hear the cries
  Of Nature's anthems gently rise,
And dream of never-fading springs,
  Beneath the Pines!

IN LOTUS LAND.

IN Lotus Land the lazy beams
  Fall slothfully, the dawdling streams
  Creep sluggishly from hill to sea,
  And sweet oblivion sleepily
The soul from toil and care redeems.

No guilt or guile of sinful themes,
No glare of Passion's lurid gleams,
  Turns innocence to misery,
    In Lotus Land.

O Life, where love unsated seems,
Where savage wrong triumphant teems,
  Where all unwelcome things that be
  Bring deathless tears and woes to thee,
Forsake thy cares and clasp thy dreams
    In Lotus Land!

AN EPITAPH.

ABOVE the monumented dead
    I stooped and read :

" This was a king !
    His empire was the latest :
    He ruled himself ! "

Let minstrels come and sing !
   Let monarchs call him greatest !
    Not power nor pelf,
Not glory gathered from an earthly thing,
  O man of might, can ever closely draw
  So vast a rebel to the rule of law !
  Thou wast a prince whose far dominions spread
  Before the living and beyond the dead !

LIFE'S TRINITY.

LIFE sinned in childhood, and with anguish sore
   Crept slowly outward through a hopeless way ;
Sweet love and laughter joyed its lips no more ;
   The Sword of Flame barred Eden's Yesterday !

A Saviour comes from mangers of the Beast,
   With modest bearing, clothed in coarse array,
Is without resting-place, esteemed the least,
   Thorn-crowned and crucified : He is To-day.

The tomb yields glories of God's endless power ;
   Life knows guilt lost and hope bestowed again ;
The night fades out, and morning hour by hour
   Opes wider still To-morrow's gates for men !

FORSAKEN.

LOVE one day bade us both good-bye,—
   The old, old Love that we knew so well !
Flushed with anger he could not quell,
He would not list to our lonely cry.

Oh the sorrow, the sob, and sigh !
   The ghastly horror and hate of hell !
Love one day bade us both good-bye,—
   The old, old Love that we knew so well !

Ah, we never may scale the sky
   Where the darling dreams of our fancies dwell,
   And we may never with rapture swell
Anthems caroled by hosts on high :
Love one day bade us both good-bye !

BUD AND BLOOM.

O STREAMS that change to bud and bloom,
   That bless the desert lands,
Your loving waters find their doom
   Beneath the burning sands,
But worlds of green and grasses grow
Where'er your benedictions flow !

So may the currents of mine hours
    Yield only gifts of love,
Till where they flow the fruits and flowers
    Of gladness rise above :
What though the desert be their doom,
O streams that change to bud and bloom !

THE MUSICIAN.

SHE plays ; and from her finger-tips
    Falls music little children know ;
She sings ; and from her happy lips
    Leaps laughter of the Long Ago !

Ah, singer, there is that in thine
Which breathes a music half divine,
And leaping in thy strains there seems
The voice of long-forgotten dreams,
Till life forsakes the ways of men
And laughs a careless child again !

LOVE AND DEATH.

A SHAPELESS Form through shining ways
    of light
Sped swiftly, far from Hate and Horror flown,
And where Love ruled the armied angels white
    Dropt his dread spear and climbed the golden
      throne.

"Hence, Monster," Love commanded. "Nay, not so,"
  Death answered him; "my brother, thou shalt share
Thy realms with me." And, sceptre-laden, lo,
  Transformed he stood, the fairest angel there!

DEATH.

WHERE meet the Bounded and the Boundless Good,
  A weary Soul that earth's deep anguish knew,
Faint in the falling shadows dimly stood
  And prayed the gates to let him enter through.

A thin, white Hand, scarce visible, with might
  Turned the vast hinges, and he walked alone
From Man the Mote to God the Infinite,
  Comrade of Truth and heir of the Unknown.

THE DEAD SINGER.

SWEET Music was his Church and Creed;
  He knew her chimes and loved to ring them;
The Muses, his good friends, indeed,
  Taught him their songs and how to sing them!

Who doubts that he shall know beyond
   His brothers all without endeavor,
And in their chorused anthems fond
   His happy heart shall sing forever!

THE ANGELUS.

TWO peasants, homeward from the fields of toil,
   Hear holy music in their hasty quest :
Their longings leave the sorrows of the soil,
   And sweetly wander in the vales of rest.

Not theirs the Knowledge that is Guilt and Grief!
   Not theirs the doubt that drives their God away!
Behold! In trustfulness of fond Belief,
   They bow their heads and lift their hearts to pray!

BIRTH'S MIRACLE.

FROM God's great mountains in the vast Unknown,
   A halting soul moves helpless down the slopes ;
On Time's broad portals pauses, lost and lone,
   And knocks for entrance into human hopes.

Then Love with fondest travail, in her soul
   The awful anguish that his life shall know,
Clasps firm his fingers and with calm control
   Leads him in terror to Man's ways of woe!

TWO PRAYERS.

"TEACH me to live, O Wisdom!" Thus in youth
Prayed I, ere Yearning to Resolve had grown;
"Enwreathe my brows with garlands of the Truth,
And lead my footsteps through the far Unknown!"

"Teach me to die, O Wisdom!" Thus in throes
Of pain implored I, after life's long quest;
"Lull my tired longings into sweet repose,
And hide my soul in everlasting rest!"

AMBITION.

WHERE 'S your glory, fickle Fame?
   Here 's the service that I brought you;
Here 's the worship; can I claim
   Nothing for the deeds I wrought you?

I 'm so weary; toil 's distressing;
   Sick, I scout your foolish snares;
Yet I 'd rather have your blessing
   Than the crown a monarch wears!

LOVE.

WHO knows the life of the tree?
   Who knows the life of the rose?
Who knows if the life that is moving me
   Is the life of the bud that blows?

Whatever it be, I shall call it Love
   That came to a world of woe,—
That came from the stars of the skies above
   To live in the stars below!

THE POET.

MORE than the Prophet and the Priest,
   Than Soldier, Sage, and King,
He brings to men through fast and feast
   The truths that seraphs sing;
He rules enthroned o'er Sword and Crown!
   In God's Most Holy Place,
He calls His kindest blessings down,
   And meets Him face to face!

THE MINSTREL'S POWER.

GLORY and power and place,
   And the gifts they bring,
Yield to the gladness and grace
   Of the hearts that sing,
Taught by the stars and the suns that rise
Music that murmurs of Paradise;
   For the minstrel knows
   Truths that only to him unclose.

LIFE.

TO all but wisdom and the wise,
   Life is a beggar lean and old,
Who wears large hunger in his eyes
   And shivers with the cruel cold.
But no! She reigns a princess fair,
With cheery cheeks and happy hair,
With laughters leaping from her lips,
And joys upon her finger-tips!

TRADITION.

A GIANT, many-sided, old, and great,
   Bestrode the highways where the nations grope,
Defied the sons of men with swords of hate,
   And drove them backward from the hills of hope,
Till one insurgent rebel smote him sore;
And lo, the Giant terrified no more!

THE CREATION OF ART.

A SHAPELESS Chaos void and lifeless lay
   Before a dreamer in his mighty hour;
He breathed his life between the lips of clay,
   And all the empty arteries throbbed with power;
Then, leaping at the Master mind's control,
It stood an angel with its maker's soul!

GOD'S CHILDREN.

GOD'S children, Time and Nature, build in sand
    Man's wondrous empires full of wealth and
        might,
Art's castles reared in playtime's warm delight,
But quickly scattered with unheeding hand ;
New races, nations, peoples,—what are they ?
Mere baubles fashioned in Creation's play !

IN A VOLUME OF POEMS.

STRANGER, pause where poet sings
    Music of divinest things ;
For, angelic, pure, and fair,
Something of his life is there,—
Something of his heart and soul
Where the wondrous measures roll !

HERO AND SINGER.

TEN thousand swords in battle strove,
    Ten thousand heroes felled their foes,
And Glory twines no wreaths above
    Forgotten graves where they repose ;
One singer sang his toils and tears,
And lo, he lives through endless years !

TO-DAY AND TO-MORROW.

THOUGH narrow, poor, and small,
    To-day is infinite
With possibles of might;
To-morrow, vast and all
    From Time's great shore to shore,
    Is finite evermore.

THE DEAD SEER.

THROUGHOUT the solemn wonders of the Night
    And all the gorgeous glories of the Day,
God's angels with the Wisdom of delight
    Taught him the Truth and told him what to say;
Till Mercy called him from the valleys lone,
And made him Master of the vast Unknown!

ONE SAYING.

ONE saying the centuries cherish
    And treasure again and again:
Live not in the books that perish,
    But live in the lives of men;
For the books shall cease at the set of sun,
But the lives of men,—they are never done!

TO A SINGER I NEVER SAW.

WHAT though we wander life along
    Through distant lands and gusty weather?
The finger-tips of tender song
    Shall link our dreaming souls together,
And every note I sing shall be
Sweet echoes of a voice from thee!

LIMITED.

BETWEEN the oceans of the Night,
    Life walks the narrow lands of Light;
And o'er the plains of thought and will
    The rivers of existence flow;
    Men sail the trailing streams, but know
How little of the seas they fill!

TRUTH'S MIGHTINESS.

THE sons of might that conquer here
    Win vict'ries not with wild alarms;
Truth naked, stript of sword and spear,
    Is greater than a world in arms!

SELF-MADE.

A FAITHFUL soul among the swine-herds wrought
    With patient hands, nor dreamed of higher things;
But lo! At last the nations found him, taught
    To sway the sceptres of a hundred kings!

THE DEAD WAIF.

A HELPLESS one, sin-summoned from the sky,
    A moment lingered in the ways of men;
Then God's fond mercy heard its lonely cry,
    And lo, He drew it to his heart again!

A PRAYER.

FILL up my heart, O Father, with relief
    While close I lean for comfort on Thy breast;
I, weary child, heart-broken with my grief,
    Creep in the dark and sob myself to rest!

DUTY.

DO thy best deed! It is not lost
    Though hid from Glory's gorgeous light;
    God's altar fires are just as bright
When one soul worships, as a host!

IN DIALECT.

THE FAITH CURE.

SPEAKIN' of religen now,
   I ain't posted much, en hain't
Aney idee aneyhow
   'Bout the way they make a saint
From a sinnin' sort of man
On the hallylooyer plan ;
Howsumever, I admit
It 's a good 'nuff thing to git,
When a feller 's brimmin' full
Of the kind thet 's practicull !

Now, fer instunce ! Thayre 's ole Bill
   Wimpler in the south of town ;
Got religen fit to kill,
   Hallylooyered up en down,
En let off a young cyclone
Down thayre on his prayin' bone,
Clar in sight of heaven's throne,
Sweepin' through the happy skies
On a shout thet satisfies !
Allus wuz a purty good
   Easy-goin' feller through
Thick en thin of things thet would
   Knock the end-gate outen you !
Wuz a blacksmith, Bill wuz ; stout,
Stouter, too, 'an all git out ;

Tall like ; en he wuz a man
On the spider-legged plan ;
Could jist hold a hoss, en drive
Hoss-shoes on him, sakes alive !
En when Bill grabbed holt the foot
Of some mule, en said, " Whoa, brute ! "
Makes no diff'runce whut a fool
Once wuz thet-air plegged mule,
He 'd jist bow his head, en lay
His long ears back thataway,
Tell ole Bill wuz plum clean through
Drivin' on the last blame shoe !
Mendin' plows en broke machines
   Wuz his main holt, too ; fer he
   Could with wires en tom-fool-ree,
Fans en flops en shakes en screens,
With contrapshuns, balls, en springs,
Make the most awdashus things
Run by steam er walked by hoss,
Feller ever come across !

Uster loaf with him fer days,
Meddertatin' on his ways,
En a sort of fishin' through,
   Jist to find out fer myse'f,
Whayre his money cantered to,
   En whut laid him on the shelf !

Wuzzent feared of work a bit !
   I kin hear his big anvill,
Seems to me, a-ringin' yit

'Fore the sun clumb up the hill ;
Never stopped to eat a bite
Tell the daytime quit fer night ;
But fer all, I jist declare,
Never had a cent to spare !
Pore ?   Pore don't spell it !   Pore
Ez a snake, en then some more !
Allus crowded him to git
Groc'ry bills paid up, en yit
He made lots of money, jist
Rollin' in, hand over fist !
Dident drink ner gamble, ner
Fool away his substance fer
Aney bad, ferbidden things
Made of vain imaginings ;
But he some way couldent make
Nothin' fer his pocket's sake,
But it tumbled out agin
Faster 'an he stuffed it in !

Now, us neighbors wundered some
(Neighbors will, the best of um !),
En we talked it kind of out,
How it all had come about ;
But not one knowed whut it wuz
Thet wuz botherin' Bill en—us !
But ole Bill one loafin' day,
Suddent like, which wuz his way,
Leaked the idee, I tell you,
Whut it wuz, clean through en through,
Circus, side-show, concert, too !

Sally,—thet 's his wife,—you see,
   One of them thayre womern wur,
Thinks theyr sick! How well she 'd be
   Somepin' 'ud be wrong with her,
En thayre 's one dizzease she had,—
Doctors comin'—mighty bad!
So the same of course wuz took
By the fam'bly pocket-book,
Tell it wilted like, en wur
Hunderd times ez sick ez her;
Fer she never seemed the wuss
Of her fits so dangeruss,
While it shrivelled up so thin
Nary cent wuz hidin' in!

Sally wuz a leetle, short,
Sawed-off woman,—jist thet sort;
Fat? Like pippins in the fall
   When theyr hearts of meller mursh
Dangle on the branches tall
   Waitin' fer the winds to sqursh!
When I 'd see her waddlin' by
   Swingin' arms both right en lef',—
I 'm ashamed of it, but I
   Wushed she 'd fall en bust herse'f,
En spill every orful bad
Blame dizzease she thort she had!

Kep' a cubberd full of pills,—
   Patent med'cine git-ups fer

The Faith Cure.

All new-fangled sorts of ills
   No one ever had but her!
Ev'ry pad en poultice, too,
   'Lectric things en strings en sich,
Warranted to pull her through
   From newmowny to the itch,
   Made no diff 'runce which wuz which ;
But each one 'ud, well or ill,
Make her sick en sicker still,
En jist keep her sick ; en she
Swallered all the theeory
Thet ole Naytcher's jist a school
Run fer some drug-mixin' fool,
En she put dependence in
Doctor bills en medicine !

I hain't no seerious dissent to
Doctors ; sometimes they will do,
En you like to have 'em come
'Twixt you en millennium,
En jist yank you, sick en sore,
From the happy, golden shore ;
But ef kep' about the place
All the time, they fall from grace.
When they git acquainted,— well,
Then they ruther lose theyr spell
Over me ; the plegged smell
Of theyr clothes en things about
Puts my stummick all to rout
Like the stuff they ladle out !

Sally, though, found much delight
Keepin' doctors thayre in sight
Clar from mornin' ontell night,
En she swallered down theyr stuff
Like she couldent git enough ;
So she went on quite a spell
Doct'rin' up en gittin' well,
En relapsin' back agin
Whayre she fust had started in !
Never seemed to gain but she
Lost it all, en 'en 'ud be
Wuss 'n ever ; nuthin', though,
Dang'russ like, fer all her show
En her mopin' signs of woe ;
But the neighbors' fokes, you know,
Like they will, jist shook theyr heads,
   Speckilatin' thet she 'd die
Sure some day, en be ez dead 's
   Mackerel dried up, by en by ;
En they went en worried on
   Whut 'ud Bill do in thet case
With them childern when she 's gone
   Yander to thet healthy place ;
En some feller 'lowed with her
   Jist removed, thet Bill 'ud shore
   Do lots better 'an before,
Whutsoever might occur ;
En perdicted thet the town
   Ez a health-reesort 'ud gain
   Ef she 'd break life's brickle chain ;—
Reppytation had run down

The Faith Cure.

Orful low en fur en wide
'Cause of illnesses she tried;—
En Jim Summers said he thort,
When she reached the heavenly port,
It quite doubtful ef she wur
Happy in them mansions fur
Without somepin ailin' her!

Wull, one summer, when she got
    Sort of risin' in her head,
Bile er somepin, like as not,
    En wuz railly sick, they said,
She jist had a rousin' spell!
    Kep' Bill dancin' day en night
Puttin' hot things on her, tell
    Blistered so she wuz a sight;
Had a high-jinks time; jist walked,
    Wrung her hands, en cried en cried,
Yelled en bellered out, en talked
    Days en nights of suicide!
En we thort, the way she tore,
Thet she 'd kick the bucket shore!

In the neighborhood thayre stayed
Ole Miss Watkins,—an ole maid
Er grass-widder,—don't know which;
But the fokes said she wuz rich,
En on thet account could do
Aneything she wanted to
Without people talkin'; she

In religen, too, you see,
Differed from the rest of us
In her faith rediculuss!
She believed with nary doubt
Sickness allus comes about
From our meanness croppin' out,
En good people sich as her
Never sick ner porely wur!
I remember when she took
   With newmowny onct, en lay
   Fer a week or two, they say,
With a all-fired scarey look,
Tell her feechers sot;—thet's why
Ever'body said she'd die;
But she said she wuzzent sick,—
   Jist a leetle tired wuz all,—
   En stuck to it! Wouldent call
   Aney doctor in, ner do
   Things thet people hurry to,
When they trump Death's leadin' trick;
Womern bawled aroun' a spell,
En she jawed 'em like, ontell
All at onct she got up well!
En the womern wuz thet mad,—
   Said they shorely knowed she wur
Jist pretendin' thet she had
   Some dizzease a-holt of her!
En went on so over it
Some won't reckergnize her yit,
Er speak to her hearty loud
When they meet her in a crowd!

The Faith Cure.

Now, when Sally got thet bile
   In her head, Miss Watkins come
With her sort of dusty smile,
   Runnin' resk of martyrdom ;
Tolt her ef she 'd jist believe
Nuthin' ailt her, she 'd receive
Lovin' faith, thet comes en brings
Health en healin' in its wings,
En so forth ; en Sally she,
   So deestracted with the pain,
Kind of took it in, you see,
   En she axt her to remain
En to tell her out en out
Things she never heerd about !

Now, thayre wuz thet very day
   Feller at Miss Watkins home
     Thort like she did ; en he come
Down to Wimpler's right away,
Bein 's Sally done invite
Him to cure her bile up right ;
Wuz from some place,—don't know whayre,—
Wichita, er som'ers thayre :
Wuz a priest,—er teacher,—er
Somepin womern hanker fer ;
   He jist talked to Sally good,
Rubbed her head and prayed with her,
   Tell the whole blame neighborhood
Called him looney en clean gone,
Tryin' his fool doctern on
Thet thayre woman ailin' so,—

Sich a hopeless case, you know!
Fer we knowed, through thin en thick
Sally's trade wuz bein' sick,
En we thort she 'd work it some
Spite of faith en Christendom!

Wull, sir, she jist swallered down
   All he tolt her; en her bile
   Busted in a leetle while
Arter thet; en all the town
Laughed a lot, en people said
She 'd got wuss things in her head
'An her bile had ever been;
But ef she 'd git somepin in
Thet 'ud do fer medicine,—
Somepin thet wuz ruther cheap,—
It might he'p her out a heap,
En Bill's pocket-book 'ud git
Full salvation outen it!

Ever see the mirth en might
Of a happy proselyte?
Thet wuz Sally! Tolt it quick
She wuz done with bein' sick,—
She had overcome the sin
Thet had brought dizzeases in;
En she said, en so it seemed,
Sickness wuz a thing she 'd dreamed,—
Thet she wuz not sick afore,
En she wouldent be no more;
So she throwed her bottles all,

The Faith Cure.

Full en empty, pads en strings,
Pills en plasters, wires en springs,
Sich as purfic saints condemn,—
In a basket in the hall ;
En she toted the display
To the garden right away,—
Dug a hole en buried 'em !
Said ez close to faith she 'd stick
Ez she had at bein' sick !

Things went forrard purty fast,
Soon as thet thayre bile wuz past ;
Arter Sally got her fill
En wuz cured of ev'ry ill,
Her religen tackled Bill
All to onct, en he give in,
Sayin' he wuz sick of sin,—
This wuz more 'an medicine !
Bill wuz shorely happies' one
Ever lived sence time begun
When he got religen thayre
Ez he knelt en tried a prayer ;
Like enough he wuz assured
Thet his pocket-book wuz cured,
En the doctor-bills 'ud quit
Grabbin' dollars outen it,—
En I hold it, at them rates,
Cheapes' cure in seven States !

Saw Bill jist the other day ;
He 's accumulatin' wealth

Sence they all learnt thataway
   How to keep theyrselves in health;
Bought a farm en paid the cash
   One year arter thet thayre bile
En theyr sickness went to smash;
   Wears a rich, contented smile,
Drives a kerridge big en fine,
En wears clothes ez good ez mine.
Whut ef no one else concurs
In thet faith of his en hers?
It is plain to all about
Thet his pocket-book is stout,
Healed ferever on thet day
Sally found the faith-cure way!

Ez I said I say agin,
   Speakin' of religen now,
Cure fer sickness en fer sin,—
I ain't posted much, en hain't
   Aney idee aneyhow
Whut is done to make a saint
From a sinnin' sort of man
On the hallylooyer plan;
But it's shorely somepin fine
When you git the genyouine
Payin' kind, thet's easy took
En will he'p the pocket-book,—
Fillin' all your longin's full
Of the sort thet's practicull,
En jist eaches fer the spot,
Like the kind thet Sally got!

OLE JIM HANKINS.

OLE Jim Hankins,—you knowed him—
Beas'ly awk'erd, tall, en slim,
Like the Lord had made him rough
Outen secon'-handed stuff,
En 'en seein' he'd played hob
Never finished up his job!
Uster live 'way up the crick
Whayre the woods en bresh is thick,
In a leetle cabin throwed
Over thayre along the road.
Traded hosses all the time,
   En he'd work his jaws en spout
   Haff a day er more about
Some ole hoss he thort sublime!
Aw, you knowed him! Blamedest one
Ever lived sence time begun!
Took the yaller janders some
When the tradin' season come,
En he yallered on en on
Tell his ellerkence 'uz gone,
En he couldent talk a bit;
Seems to me I see him yit
Weepin' like his heart 'uz wrung,
'Cause he couldent wag his tongue,
Like a easy-run machine,

'Bout the hosses he had seen.
Don't remember! Wull, I swow!
Why, I see the feller now!
How he lived, ez some men do,—
Ole hoss trader through en through,—
En the people fer en wide
Come to see him when he died!

Wush you could a-knowed ole Jim
'Fore the janders tackled him!

Ganglin'-like en sort of slow,
He a-hitchin' 'long 'ud go,
Er he santered 'round en lit
His ole pipe en puffed a bit:
   Swallered smoke ontell it riz
   Through thet peaked nose of his;
Hawked en hawked, en 'en he 'd spit,
Tell he 'd wet en kind of spile,
In his free en easy style,
'Bout a front yard full of ground
Thet wuz layin' thayre around;
Er he 'd take his yaller twist
Of terbacker in his fist,
En sock in his teeth, en pull
Tell his mouth wuz brimmin' full;
Then he 'd work his nimble jaw
Up en down acrost the chaw
In his happy, keerless way,
Fer the likes of haff a day!
Uster be the bigges' fun,

Jist to set en watch him squirt
Juicy mouth-fulls at the dirt,
Like some long, infernal gun
Would its buzzin' bullets throw
At the breast-works of a foe;
Whew, but he could spit it hard!
Hit a bull's-eye twenty yard,
En wuz never knowed to miss
When he squoze them lips of his!

Wush you could a-knowed ole Jim
'Fore the janders tackled him!

Uster dress the queeres', too!
Wore the bigges' size of shoe,—
Number ten er thayreabout,—
With his toes a-stickin' out;
Said he 'd turned 'em out fer grass
With the horned, four-footed class!
Round-a-bout en overhalls
Kivered shins en sunken breast,
En his hick'ry shirt wuz best
To pertect him from the squalls,
Ragin' storms 'en winds thet blowed
On the wintry ways he knowed;
En upon his head of hair,
Shaggy-like, he 'd allus wear
His ole cap of coon-skin hide
With the fur on outer side,
En the striped'st tail you 'd find
Stickin' proudly out behind,

Bobbin' up en down on high
Like a banner in the sky!
　Never had a gallus on,
Ner a collar ner a tie ;
　Said his natchurl way 'd be gone
Ef he 'd wear them horrid things,—
Frills en furbelows en strings,—
Thet the han'some fellers git
When they spark en spruce a bit;
En his whiskers long en rough
Suited him jist good enough,
Ef terbacker juice got in
Ez it wundered down his chin!

Wush you could a-knowed ole Jim
'Fore the janders tackled him!

Beat'nes' feller ever seen!
Allus puzzled my machine
How ole Hankins got so smart
In the tradin'-hosses art.
Fokes called him a kind of fool
　Thet in manners couldent shine,—
　But in his peculeyer line
He wuz born to run en rule ;
Never had a word to say
　When jist common things en sich,
　Very pore er very rich,
Come around his lonesome way ;
　Never knowed jist which wuz which ;
But when some new hoss wuz by,

Spread his mouth en let 'er fly !
Whut he knowed about a hoss,
   Hosses' ages, ways, en looks,
   Would a-filled a dozen books
No man ever come across !
Never seen him downed er beat
   When you took him in his line,
   Fer a man had best resign
When he tried to work a cheat
On ole Hankins, 'bout the worth
Of the hosses of the earth ;
En regardin' his own trade
He wuz allus thayre,—en stayed !

Wush you could a-knowed ole Jim
'Fore the janders tackled him !

But he had a heart ez kind
   Ez the womern folks, en wide
   Ez the wants onsatisfied
Thet upon our paths we find ;
Nary kid in all the land
   But a-shoutin' loud 'ud run
Fer to grab him by the hand,
   With a heart as full of fun
Ez a—millon is of juice
When a feller lets it loose !
Sacks of candy en sich things
   Fer which babies raise a row,—
Tops en marvels, knives en strings,—
   In his pockets wuz, somehow ;

People allus welcomed Jim
To theyr homes en honored him,
Like he wuz a king of might
Thet wuz fetchin' 'em delight !
None thayre wuz but he would do
Level best to pull 'em through,
En they allus praised en blest
Whut he did, like all possest !
Carried widder womern flour,
Wood, en vittles, by the hour,
En wuz like a daddy to
Orphan kids the country through.
Never saved his money, though,—
Fellers like him don't, you know !
Never keered fer pride er pelf
Ner a copper fer hisself,
But the best man happ'nin' round
On the top side of the ground,—
Give the last blame cent he had
Jist to make some feller glad !

Wush you could a-knowed ole Jim
'Fore the janders tackled him !

Led a sort of lonesome life,
 Ez some fokes remarked of Jim ;
Never found the stripe of wife
 Thet 'ud jist agree with him ;
Though the older settlers say
 Thet when he wuz but a boy
 Clean chuck-full of purfic joy,

He 'd a sweet heart glad en gay,
But she pined away en died,
Leavin' him onsatisfied,
En through all the seasons grum
His pore heart a vacuum !
No relations of his own,
Walked the ways thet he had known,—
   Cows, ner pigs, ner other fokes ;
Fer he allus lived alone,
   Chawed terbacker, told his jokes ;
Took things jist ez easy thayre
Ez he could most aney whayre,
Like a 'coon of highes' type
When the roas'in' ears is ripe !
His ole dawg en hoss wuz all
   Thet he keered to have about,
En he kep' them in his call
   Jist to sort of he'p him out
When he got to feelin' blue
En not knowin' whut to do !
But at feller-mortals he
Drawed the line, ez all could see,
   Though he never harmed a man
Fer ez I have ever heerd,
En he never wuz afeerd
Of his shadder, ner could be ;
   Fer he took the gospel plan,
En he made hisself as good
Ez he wushed his fellers would,—
Jist ez good ez good could be,
Ez he allus seemed to me !

Wush you could a-knowed ole Jim
'Fore the janders tackled him!

But when Jim got sick in bed,
   En ole Death with floppin' wings
Hovered all around his head,
   En the darkes' kinds of things
Come around whayre he wuz spread,—
Seemed to me the earth en sky
'Ud be blackened by en by!
Saddes' sight you ever seed,—
Railly made my ole heart bleed,—
When he rared up kind of weak
On his elbow, fer to speak,
En he said: "I never keer
How the Lord may treat me here,
But it strikes me ruther bad
En it makes me sort of sad,
'Cause I've got to go away
Whayre the juice-harps allus play,
Whayre no hosses trot before,
En hoss-traders trade no more;
But ef I could trade agin
'Fore I leave the trails of sin,
I could pass my checks, en know
Work wuz over here below!"

Wull, sir, when he once got through,
   All the people thayre jist cried,
Bellered out en blubbered, too,
   Like the whole creation 'd died;

But I—stepped—right up—to—Jim—
  Knowin' whut he wanted most;
Traded hosses thayre with him
  'Fore his consciousness wuz lost
(Made ten dollars; only time
Jim got euchered on a dime!),
En acrost the river he
Peaceful like en quietly
Waded through the worters deep,
Like a youngster gone to sleep!
En ef heaven is over thayre
Whayre them angel bein's air,
I 'm jist shore 't wuz made fer Jim
En all fellers good ez him!

Wush you could a-knowed ole Jim
'Fore the janders tackled him!

THE BANKS OF TURKEY RUN.

LIKE a thousen birds of brightness from the isles
    of summer seas,
Rickollections full of gladness come with songs en
    lullabies,
En I listen to the carols thet with gentle voices roll
Full of tenderness en beauty down upon my weary
    soul;
Fer thayre 's one thet keeps a-singin' with a song
    thet 's never done,
En I see the bendin' willers on the banks of Turkey
    Run!

En agin I be a youngster with a youngster's foolin'
   dreams,
With his highfalutin' notions, en his fiddle-faddle
   schemes
With the laughin' en the cryin', with the sorrer en
   the joy,
Thet is jumbled up together in the bosom of a boy ;
En agin my airly fancies in a fairy loom air spun
Underneath the dancin' shadders on the banks of
   Turkey Run.

En agin I be a school-boy with the other merry lads,
When Joe en Jerry, Bill en I wuz only leetle tads,—
When a half a dozen marvels en a kivered ball wuz
   worth,
With a knife of Barlow pattern, all the treasures of
   the earth ;
En the soundin' sort of thunder from a poppin'
   kind of gun
Sot our faces all a-giggle on the banks of Turkey
   Run.

It 'ud tickle aney feller jist to see the solemn look,
When the master wuz a-watchin', thet we fastened
   on the book ;
But the mischief stickin' in us, like pertaters in a sack,
It wuz never hard to empty when the teacher
   turned his back !
O, the paper wads we tumbled thet 'ud weigh about
   a ton,
In thet crazy-cornered school-house on the banks
   of Turkey Run !

The Banks of Turkey Run.

How we uster chase the robins en the rabbits in the woods,
How we gethered bloomin' posies in the sighin' solitudes!
How we wundered all the medders in our roamin's o'er en o'er,
How we teetered in the branches of the beech en sycamore!
Er we watched the rompin' minners ez they rassled in theyr fun,
While we nearly bust a-laughin', on the banks of Turkey Run!

How we uster go a-fishin', when the day wuz gittin' late,
With a bent pin fer a fish-hook en a fish-worm fer a bait!
With a leetle line of cotton en a hazel fer a pole,
How we sought the softes' places by the wides', deepes' hole!
How we tee-hee-ed at the nibbles, caught the fishes one by one,
With the bigges' kind of prowess, on the banks of Turkey Run!

When the sun wuz burnin' shavin's in the heatin' stove of June,
En the clock upon the mantel wuz a-knockin' off the noon;
When the beams in bunches blistered as they never did afore,

En the sweat wuz drippin', droppin', from the
    mouth of every pore,
How we skipped acrost the medders, how our swim-
    min' wuz begun
In the cool en crystal waters 'tween the banks of
    Turkey Run !

O, the smilin' days of childhood ! O, the loudly-
    laughin' years !
When contentment brings the moments nary trace
    of toils er tears !
When the pleasures jine the longin's en the fairy
    fingers roll
All theyr heaps of angel music in upon the blazin'
    soul !
O, my Joe, en Bill, en Jerry ! Trustin' comrades,
    you wuz won
Whayre my bare feet brushed the grasses on the
    banks of Turkey Run !

O, them airly ties air busted ! But I offen wait en
    weep
Whayre the pleasures of my boyhood in theyr leetle
    cradles sleep,
Rocked by angel hands of glory full of gladness
    onexpressed,
Tell theyr eyes air soothed to slumber by the lul-
    labies of rest ;
Yit I sometimes like to wake 'em, jist to see theyr
    foolish fun,
Back through all the dismal shadows, to the banks
    of Turkey Run !

En alas! Thayre wuz another! She wuz fairer
    than the rest,
En she allus had a hearin' fer the wushes of my
    breast,—
Allus wuz a chunk of sunshine en a piece of quiet
    glee,
Allus had a smile of welcome en a tender word fer
    me;
En without her wuz no shinin', en of happiness
    wuz none
Rompin' through them days of childhood on the
    banks of Turkey Run.

O, her home wuz in a cottage whayre the mornin'-
    glories hung,
En the airly birds of Aprile with theyr sweetes'
    music sung!
Thayre wuz roses 'round her winder, thayre wuz
    roses 'round her door,
Thet wuz stickin' full of blushes, but they seemed
    to blush the more
When her eyes wuz seen a-peepin', en her cheeks
    shone like the sun
From thet cozy leetle cottage on the banks of Tur-
    key Run!

Many en many a time we wundered in the grassy
    medder-land
With our wishes thayre together en our longin's
    hand in hand;

How we dreamed about the future, when the world
    should give me fame,
En when she would be thrice noble to be worthy
    of my name!
Thus we dreamed en thus we fancied; others might
    my boyhood shun,
But I found her kind, my sweetheart, on the banks
    of Turkey Run!

But the times have been a-changin' sence them airly
    years of joy
When she wuz jist a leetle girl en I a leetle boy,—
When Joe en Jerry, Bill en I, together wuz at play,
With our hearts ez light ez feathers every minute of
    the day,
En at twilight sunk to slumber tell the mornin' wuz
    begun
In the gloomy, silent forests on the banks of Turkey
    Run!

Bill en Joe have gone a-rovin' on a fortune-huntin'
    quest
Through the silver mines en Injuns in the mount-
    ings of the West;
But the janders come to Jerry with a solemn sort
    of call,
Tell they painted him ez yaller ez a punkin in the
    fall;
En to-day I saw his tombstone ez it glittered in the
    sun
Over in the leetle churchyard, on the banks of
    Turkey Run!

En, alas, my precious sweetheart! Like a posy-blossom white
Did she slowly fade en wither, tell her spirit took its flight!
Like an angel into heaven did she slowly, calmly creep,
Tell her lovely life wuz over en her longin's went to sleep;
En the tollin', tollin' church-bells dropt the dirges one by one
Ez we laid her by the willer on the banks of Turkey Run!

Thayre a leetle cross of marble marks the silent, sacred shade
Whayre the blossom en the beauty of my ole sweetheart is laid;
En the summer has a sadness thet is cryin' through the years,
En my heart is full of sorrer en my eyes air full of tears;
Fer I 've allus had a failin', sence her friendship fust I won,
Fer thet lovin' leetle maiden, on the banks of Turkey Run!

But them days air past ferever in the years of Long Ago,
En a wishin' to be wealthy has enraptured Bill en Joe;
Death has taken Jerry; only I, of all the boys,

Am remainin' to remember all them airly angel
    joys ;
But to-night I see theyr faces ez they peep in full of
    fun,
En agin we 're boys together, on the banks of
    Turkey Run !

MORALIZIN'S.

THAYRE 'S nuthin' in the world thet 's haff
    So full of comfort as a laff,
En nuthin' like a healthy grin
To make a feller glad agin !

It ain't the weepin' sort of chap
Thet goes a-groanin' when the crap
Of wheat is provin' kind of small
En corn gits frost-bit in the fall,
Who never finds a thing amiss
Er gits the bigges' hunks of bliss !

I uster know a feller-man
Thet seemed to foller sich a plan ;
Fer it wuz his besettin' pride
To keep hisself onsatisfied,
En nuthin' ever come en fit
Eggsackly ez he wanted it.
When purfic joys wuz standin' by,
He 'd jist go off alone, en try
To stuff the sweet en shinin' days
With sorrers all contrairy ways ;

Moralizin'.

En when the times wuz purty tough,
It seemed he couldent cry enough,
But magnified his leetle keers,
En wushed he wuz a bar'l of tears,
Close by the sea, to tumble in
En never find hisself agin !

He allus stuffed his place fer brains
A-heapin' up with woes en pains,
En had a pile of his own sense
A-savin' up fer Providence ;
Fer he had plannin's mighty nice,
En could a-give the Lord advice
About the way to hold the strings
En git the purfic run of things !

But somehow fellers sich as him
Have chances thet is kind of slim
At findin' in these narrer years
A han'kerchief fer all theyr tears ;
Fer in the purty strains of song
Thayre 's allus notes a-goin' wrong,
En summer showers have allus growed
A mud-hole in the smoothes' road.

'Cause somepin goes a leetle bad
Hain't aney reason to be sad,
For thayre is heerd a thousen songs
To every dozen of our wrongs,
En it makes trouble deeper yit
To bawl en blubber over it !

A man had better laff en grin
En fetch the pleasures back agin,
When life is lookin' kind of black
En loads git heavy on his back,
Fer things air shore to have theyr way
Whatever he kin do er say!

To gether up the joys thet bless
These human days with happiness,
En larn to take things ez they come,
Has allus been the bigges' sum
Thet ever made a mortal wet
His throbbin' brain with hones' sweat;
It 's sort of strange, but yit our keers
Git leetler with the passin' years,
En rale old fokes air apt to find
Theyr discontentments quite resigned;
Fer him thet knows the blessed art
Of garnerin' pleasures in his heart,
Gits happy, tell he thinks he must
Jist sure en sartin go en bust,
Too joyous fur to keep en hold
The laffs none ever bought fer gold!

A feller mussent hope to find
Things jest a'cordin' to his mind,
Fer naytcher with her star en sun
Wuz shorely made fer more 'an one,
En number seven shoes won't suit
The natcherl size of every foot,
En whut 'll make a dozen glad,

Ez like ez not 'll make one sad ;
But fer myse'f I calkilate
Thet man is master of his fate ;
En well I know fer man en boy
This world is heapin' up with joy,
En all we do to git enough
Is, jist grab han'fuls of the stuff
En cram our longin' bosoms full
Of gladness irresistabull,
Tell him thet laughs en grins the best
Gits bigger blisses 'an the rest !

"'FORE WILLYUM WRIT A BOOK."

'FORE Willyum Wilkins writ a book,
    We allus called him Bill, fer short,
En hardly give a secon' look
    At him beyant the common sort ;
Fer he wuz one of us, en we
    Jist never thort he 'd ever do
Some big, oncommon thing, en be
    Renownin' all the country through.

I met him fust one rainy night
    When fast 1 rid my ole hoss Dick
Kersplash to town with all my might,
    En brung the doctor purty quick ;
En when we got back, in her lap
    My wife wuz holdin' him, by zook !
A most onlikely leetle chap,—
    'Fore Willyum writ a book.

I knowed him when he uster be
    A leetle freckled cuss thet wur
Same ez the boys belonged to me,—
    No purtier ner likelier;
With britches rolled up, fixed complete,
    En ole straw hat no pup 'ud hook,
En big stone-bruises on his feet,—
    'Fore Willyum writ a book!

But now he's got a great big name,—
    Bill's growed to Willyum mighty quick,
En with the purty gal called Fame
    They say he's gittin' orful thick;
But he ain't happier now instid,
    Than when fer city ways he shook
The home thet smiles ez smile it did,
    'Fore Willyum writ a book!

He wears a long-tail coat, en curls,
    En tall plug-hats, en spotted ties,
Talks through his nose at painted girls
    Thet wear gold glasses on theyr eyes;
But I jist know his soul don't sing
    Ez glad en free ez when he took
The cows to pasture in the spring,—
    'Fore Willyum writ a book!

En some fool college 'way down East
    Has doctored him an LL.D.,
En all sich fol-de-rol,—at least,
    Jake Johnson tells the same to me;
I s'pose he hardly knows the fokes
    He uster, 'fore us he forsook

To dawdle 'round with city blokes,—
  'Fore Willyum writ a book!

They say them big bugs do him proud;
  He hobbies with the good en great,
En jist enthooses every crowd
  Comes out to hear him speckilate;
But somehow I can't picture him
  'Cept as a boy down by the brook,
A-fishin' in the shadders dim,—
  'Fore Willyum writ a book!

En should I meet him som'ers now,
  Ole times 'ud pore my bosom full
Of them ole things, en on my brow
  Romp glories irresistabull;
With quiverin' lip en teary lid
  I'd grab his hand with happy look,—
Shout "Howdy, Bill!" as shout I did
  'Fore Willyum writ a book!

"WHEN THE ROAS'IN'-EARS IS PLENTY."

TALK about the joys of winter! Whut's the
    fun of foolin' round
With the posies dead en buried, en the snows upon
    the ground?
When the wind's a-tossin' blizzards in a most dis-
    tressin' way
Tell you have to set a-straddle of the fire-place all
    the day!

But I tell ye life's a-livin' when the summer grows
  the grass
Over all the nooks en crannies whayre a feller's feet
  kin pass,
En the whole world seems of heaven but a half for-
  gotten type,
When the roas'in'-ears is plenty en the worter-
  millons ripe!

Roas'in'-ears is best of eatin', though not very much
  fer style,—
Shuck an armfull fer yer dinner, sot 'em on en let
  'em bile;
Salt 'em well, en smear some butter on the juicy
  cobs ez sweet
Ez the lips of maple-sugar thet yer sweetheart has
  to eat!
Talk about ole Mount Olympus en the stuff them
  roosters spread
On theyr tables when they feasted,—nectar drink,
  ambrosia bread!
Why, I tell ye, fellers, never would I swop the grub
  I swipe
When the roas'in'-ears is plenty en the worter-mil-
  lons ripe!

Near the sugar-camps of glory is the worter-millon
  patch,
Like a great big nest of goodies thet is jist a-gone
  to hatch;

En ye take yer thumb en finger in an ecstasy so
   drunk
Thet ye hardly hear the music of theyr dreamy
   plunky-plunk !
En the griefs air gone ferever, en the sorrers lose
   control
Ez ye feed the angel in ye on the honeys of a soul,
En ye smack yer lips with laughter while the birds
   of heaven pipe,—
When the roas'in'-ears is plenty en the worter-mil-
   lons ripe !

O, the darlin' days of summer when the stars of
   plenty shine
With the apples in the orchard en the grapes upon
   the vine ;
When the hedges bud en blossom, en the medders
   rich en rare
Breathe the perfume of the clovers like an incense
   everywhayre !
En the world seems like yer mother, with the tender
   hands thet bless
All the restless race of struggle with a heaped-up
   happiness,
En her han'kerchiefs of gladness from yer eyes the
   weepin's wipe,
When the roas'in'-ears is plenty en the worter-mil-
   lons ripe !

"PUT 'ER THAYRE FER NINETY DAYS!"

WULL, ole Jim! of all the strays!
Put 'er thayre fer ninety days!
Glad to see ye! Whayre ye been
Sence ye last come rollin' in?
How's yer fokes? en leetle Jim,—
Whut about the gals en him?
Tell me all in quickes' phrase,—
Put 'er thayre fer ninety days!

Put 'er thayre fer ninety days!
How it warms my heart to raise
To yer face my happy eyes
En to hear yer kind replies!
It's put near a life-time sence
You en me saw them events
Thet return through cloud en haze,—
Put 'er thayre fer ninety days!

Put 'er thayre fer ninety days,
While upon yer face I gaze!
Not changed much sence we wuz boys
Thinkin' mischief most of joys;
Older some en sobered some
By the jolty roads ye've come,

"Put 'er Thayre fer Ninety Days!"

But yer tender naytcher stays,—
Put 'er thayre fer ninety days!

Put 'er thayre fer ninety days!
Yes, life is a tangled maze,
Full of sorrers en of songs,
Cryin's, laffin's, rights, en wrongs;
But from fountains of distress
Bubble streams of happiness,
En the stars in darkness blaze,—
Put 'er thayre fer ninety days!

Put 'er thayre fer ninety days!
Whut ye sayin'? Joy betrays,—
Fam'bly dead? En leetle Jim?
Gals en mother dead with him!
O, my own heart, pardner, knows
Somepin of the deepes' woes!
Yit fer all its grief, life pays,—
Put 'er thayre fer ninety days!

Put 'er thayre fer ninety days!
Let yer hand be one thet stays;
Pitch yer tent en camp with me
All the years thet yit shall be!
Love shall heal yer heart, en bring
Music fer us both to sing,
En our tears 'll roll in praise,—
Put 'er thayre fer ninety days!

Put 'er thayre fer ninety days!
Wisdom wreathes us with her bays,
En around our lives entwine
Lessons thet air shore devine!
En we 'll live,—yes, live,—en love
Tell the Father up above
Grabs our hands in his, en says,
" Put 'er thayre fer ninety days!"

AT FWEDDIE'S.

I LIKE Fweddie mighty well!
    Fweddie 's got a dog what plays
Hide en seek, en he can tell
    Whare you go to, funniest ways!
He ist puts his paws up thare
    'Crost his eyes en shets 'em tight,
Tell he comes en hunts you whare
    You are hided out of sight!

He can play ball, too, en fetch
    What you say fer him to bring,—
Jump into the pond, en ketch
    Sticks en hats en ever'thing!
Gits 'em in his mouth en takes
    Races 'round a time er two,
En he barks, en shakes en shakes
    Dirty worter over you!

At Fweddie's.

Fweddie's pony 's Tiddle-wink ;
    Littlust one you ever see !
Cuter 'n Curly, too, I think,—
    Only 'bout as high as me !
Me en him got on en rode,—
    Bofe togever ist like one,—
Didunt make much of a load,
    En wuz ist the mostest fun !

Fweddie hit 'im wiv a stick,
    Right thare by the worter-trough,
En the pony tried to kick
    Up his heels en throw us off !
Then he run en run, tell we
    Got purshed off by that big limb,—
Fweddie said 'at some time he
    'D ride the meanness out of him !

I like Fweddie,—yes, I do,
    Mighty well, en Fweddie he
En his dog en pony, too,
    Thinks a orful sight of me ;
En when all of us git out
    Havin' fun en bein' glad,
We ist know a heap about
    Goodest times boys ever had !

L'ENVOI.

I HAVE sung you a song
   Whether worthy or not,
Whether righteous or wrong;
I have sung you a song
Whether little or long;
   Though it soon be forgot,
I have sung you a song
   Whether worthy or not!

www.ingramcontent.com/pod-product-compliance
Lightning Source LLC
Chambersburg PA
CBHW020857230426
43666CB00008B/1222